BLOOD OF THE LAMB CATHOLIC BIBLE STUDY

To Bud & Pat,

With love,

God Bless,

Beth

BLOOD OF THE LAMB CATHOLIC BIBLE STUDY

SHED SEVEN TIMES TO SAVE US

BETH LEONARD

authorHOUSE®

AuthorHouse™ LLC
1663 Liberty Drive
Bloomington, IN 47403
www.authorhouse.com
Phone: 1-800-839-8640

Published by AuthorHouse   03/14/2014

ISBN: 978-1-4918-7223-9 (sc)
ISBN: 978-1-4918-7222-2 (hc)
ISBN: 978-1-4918-7224-6 (e)

Library of Congress Control Number: 2014904651

Imprimatur
The Archdiocese of Indianapolis
Nihil Obstat: Rev. Dennis M. Duvelius, MA, VF
Censor Librorum
Imprimatur: Most Rev. Christopher J. Coyne, S.L.D.
Vicar General/Moderator of the Curia

The **Nihil Obstat** *and* **Imprimatur** are official declarations that a book or pamphlet is free of doctrinal or moral error. No implication is contained therein that those who have granted the **Nihil Obstat** and **Imprimatur** agree with the contents, opinions, or statements expressed.

Dedication

My family has grown since my last book, and also my blessings!

To Bill, Sarah, and Moira—the originals

To Kyle, Kevin, and grandson Cayden—the newbies
ww
Thank you for your support and love

Acknowledgments

Imprimatur
The Archdiocese of Indianapolis
Nihil Obstat: Rev. Dennis M. Duvelius, MA, VF
Censor Librorum
Imprimatur: Most Rev. Christopher J. Coyne, S.L.D.
Vicar General/Moderator of the Curia

The **Nihil Obstat** and **Imprimatur** are official declarations that a book or pamphlet is free of doctrinal or moral error. No implication is contained therein that those who have granted the **Nihil Obstat** and **Imprimatur** agree with the contents, opinions, or statements expressed.

Bible excerpts are included with permission:
Scripture texts in this work are taken from the New American Bible, revised edition © 2010, 1991, 1986, 1970 Confraternity of Christian Doctrine, Washington, D.C. and are used by permission of the copyright owner. All Rights Reserved. No part of the New American Bible may be reproduced in any form without permission in writing from the copyright owner.

Catholic Link boxes are taken with permission from the *Catechism of the Catholic Church*:
English translation of the Catechism of the Catholic Church for the United States of America copyright © 1994, United States Catholic Conference, Inc.—Libreria Editrice Vaticana. English translation of the Catechism of the Catholic Church: Modifications from the Editio Typica copyright © 1997, United States Catholic Conference, Inc.—Libreria Editrice Vaticana.

Excerpts from the Catholic Liturgy:
Excerpts from the English translation of *The Roman Missal* © 2010, International Commission on English in the Liturgy Corporation. All rights reserved.

Beth Leonard

Special Thanks

Julie Crowe, a dear and very smart friend of mine, took the time to read, review and edit this book. Her input and suggestions for improving the flow were invaluable to me. She spent many hours of her own time pouring through rough drafts while making notes for improvement. Julie not only shared her editing talents with me but, as a convert to Catholicism as an adult, she was also able to add a wonderfully spiritual perspective to our discussions. The book is better because she took the time to help me. I am grateful.

Specialty Artwork

Laura Liotti, an artist from Indianapolis, Indiana, has allowed her depictions of "The blood of the Lamb" to be used on the cover and throughout this book. Her pictures include: Front Cover portrait of The Lamb of God, The Agony in the Garden artwork, and The Scourging artwork. Not only is Laura a dear friend but also she helps me gain a visual for the words I write. It is true that one picture can say a thousand words. Laura also painted the beautiful portrait of Mary on the cover of my first book, *The Seven Sorrows Bible Study for Catholics, What We Can Learn from Our Mother of Sorrows*. Thank you Laura, for once again sharing your artistic talents and passion for Jesus through these paintings. Please view other artwork of Laura's on her website: LauraLiotti.com

Foreword

Open the newspaper, turn on the television, visit the movie theater, everywhere there is talk of blood. Everywhere there is talk of vampires and the undead. The bottom line of all the blood is clear, to scare us and frighten us.

Beth Leonard's book is in stark contrast to all the fear and gore. The core message of her inspiring book is this: God in the person of Jesus loved us so much that he came to be with us; to shed blood for us. An old time evangelist once said, "Most Christians have enough religion to make themselves miserable." The religion advocated by Beth is rooted in the Latin origin of the word. It "binds us together" in celebration of God's love. It "binds us together" to be challenged by God's love.

Beth Leonard employs the powerful combination of catechesis, prayer, discussion and old-fashioned storytelling to enrich our lives. Pope Francis has said, "I have a dogmatic certainty of this: God is in every person's life." Beth shows us how Jesus' shedding blood is not just an event centuries old but an event ever new in each of our lives.

Reverend Robert Sims, STL, MA
"Fr. Bob"

Introduction to
The Blood of the Lamb
Catholic Bible Study

On the evening of Thursday October 9, 2008 I attended a dinner and speaker event at St. Luke Parish in Indianapolis, Indiana. Beside each of our plates sat a laminated tri-fold holy card containing two beautiful prayers. The first prayer, on The Seven Sorrows of Mary, was very familiar to me. In fact, Our Blessed Mother's sorrows became the inspiration for my first Bible Study. The second prayer was completely new to me. It was a twelve-year daily novena based on the seven times Jesus shed his precious blood for us. I read through the prayer that night and felt called to begin the novena.

Although my twelve-year commitment will end on October 8, 2020, I doubt I will ever stop praying this prayer. To me, it would be like choosing to stop snacking and I REALLY enjoy "food-grazing" throughout the day! Maybe that is why I like this prayer so much; I kind of "snack" on it all day. Usually I say one of the seven devotions before I rise from bed, and a few more in the afternoon and evening. Anything left over gets added to my bedtime prayers. Whatever time my day allows—a quick two-minute meditation all the way to a several hour study—the "blood of the Lamb" that saved us always enriches my day. It has become the part of my day I look forward to most because I get to spend time with Jesus.

Many times one of the seven blood-shedding occurrences will cause me to think about someone who needs prayer. Sometimes it provides a message of humility designed for me. Meditating on them is sometimes sad, in a thankful kind of way, but mostly it is just peaceful and reassuring.

In researching the Precious Blood of Jesus, an interesting trail of dedications arose. It seems that the early fathers of the Church fully recognized the significance of a devotion to the Most Precious Blood of Our Lord Jesus Christ, for it is his blood that is ransomed for our salvation. Pope Pius IX, in 1849, asked that the month of July be dedicated to the Feast of the Precious Blood of our Lord. Ten years later, he formalized his request by decreeing the feast be celebrated across the Universal Church. Still growing in momentum, Pope Pius X assigned the first day of July as the chosen feast day of celebration for all churches when remembering the Precious Blood of Jesus. Through an Apostolic letter of Pope John XXIII (1958-1963), he again encouraged and promoted the devotion to the Most Precious Blood of our Lord Jesus Christ. It was not until after the changes in the liturgy following Vatican II (1962-1965) that the feast was no longer mandated throughout the universal church. Many parish priests, at their own discretion, still choose to celebrate this devotion in July.

This book is a compilation of my bible research, interviews with others, lessons I have learned by opening myself up to the wise teaching of Jesus, and meditative thoughts I have acquired. Although the book is designed for group reflection (see "Discussion Corners" in each chapter) it may, just as easily, be used for individual study and reflection.

This Bible study is written especially for Catholics because I am gratefully indebted to the teaching of the Roman Catholic Church. It is difficult to imagine a world without its presence, traditions and discipline. The more one studies the "Universal" and "Apostolic" Roman Catholic Church, the more one appreciates its great antiquity and the rules that were established to preserve its treasure for all generations. We are a better world because of its steadfast and unwavering moral doctrine. The seed of Jesus Christ rooted itself in the hearts of the apostles and they led our way to discovering the new covenant of Christianity. So solid is the tree that grew from their sacrifice that we all might find rest and solace within its sturdy branches.

Within this Bible Study, you will find references to our holy Mass and *Catechism of the Catholic Church* (Catholic link sections). The links were placed within each chapter to help us discern the teachings of the Catholic Church in reference to what we are studying. The Bible used for all scripture passages and reference is The New American Bible.

The seven times Jesus shed his precious blood for mankind
The Circumcision
The Agony in the Garden
The Flogging
The Crowning of Thorns
The Carrying of the Cross
The Crucifixion
The Piercing in the Side

How to pray this prayer: Say the 1st devotion, *The Circumcision*, while asking God to enlighten you about its mystery. A simple prayer like this will do, "Today, dear Lord, what do you want me to know about this devotion?" Repeat as many times as needed to purposefully clear your mind of all other thoughts and begin to open your heart and mind to new and endless lessons. Pray one Our Father and one Hail Mary.
Repeat with the remaining six devotions.
Be enlightened.

Our Father

Our Father, Who art in heaven,
hallowed be Thy name;
Thy kingdom come;
Thy will be done on earth as it is in heaven.
Give us this day our daily bread;
and forgive us our trespasses
as we forgive those who trespass against us;
and lead us not into temptation,
but deliver us from evil. Amen.

Hail Mary

Hail Mary, full of grace. The Lord is with thee.
Blessed art thou amongst women,
and blessed is the fruit of thy womb, Jesus.
Holy Mary, Mother of God,
pray for us sinners,
now and at the hour of our death. Amen.

Contents

The Circumcision

Bible passages needed for study of this chapter:

Luke 2:21	Acts 7:51-52	Genesis 17:15-20
Genesis 17:1-14	1 Corinthians 7:17-20	Genesis 18:12-15
Jeremiah 4:1-4	Galatians 6:14-15	

For the circumcision of Christ, please read Luke 2:21.

That was short and to the point, wasn't it? Okay, close the book, end of chapter—or is there more to discover in Luke's slight but powerful passage? Does a deeper message lie within these words, beyond the customary practice of circumcision and beyond the simple naming of a child? What does Jesus ask us to learn from these verses and how did God foretell this moment and build our understanding over the years of teachings found in the Old Testament? Let's look closer to find not only the hidden meaning, but also the beauty in which this passage comes to be a significant starting point for our faith as Christians. Even our names are, as was the naming of Jesus, blessed and important to God.

In reviewing Luke 2:21, it is important to note that Joseph and Mary were following Jewish custom (established by God in Genesis 17:12) when they had eight-day old Jesus circumcised. Also, the name brought forth on this day was predestined. The name of Jesus was first brought to Mary by the angel Gabriel whom God sent prior to conception (Luke 1:26) and was then announced again to Joseph in a dream (Matthew 2:21). However, the first time the name "Jesus" would have publicly been declared would have been during this holy ceremony, signifying the covenant between God and man. From His heavenly throne God orchestrated the actions, words and timing for His angels to appear on Earth to guide (and name) His salvation plan.

How do you think God's angels marked these days on their heavenly calendars? Did they leap for joy, sing great hymns of praise or blast their trumpets with the triumphant news? The promised Savior was on his way! The mother was chosen, the father advised and the child born. But it was not until the day of his circumcision that the child would be lawfully given his name and it forever written into time. There would be no turning back. Each earthly day would pass as all of heaven took notice and rejoiced in the strength, wisdom and handiwork of their God, now inherited by and thriving in His only Son, Jesus Christ.

CIRCUMCISION IN THE OLD AND NEW TESTAMENTS

We do not have to read far into the Bible before the Covenant of Circumcision is established. We find it in the first book of the Bible, Genesis. In Chapter 17 God appeared to Abram with a specific purpose in mind. He desired a covenant to mark the close relationship between Abram (including his household and descendants) and their One True God. Let's read it to determine the ground rules. Open to Genesis 17:1-14 and read the story that became the "Covenant of Circumcision" and the beginning of the 12 tribes of Israel that would follow God throughout the Old Testament and serve as a human chain, linking finally to the birth of Our Lord Jesus Christ.

In verse 2 God speaks of establishing a covenant with him and then He says He will make numerous Abram's descendants. To date, however, ninety-nine year old Abram had no legitimate children and only one son named Ishmael, born to him 13 years prior by his wife's maidservant named Hagar. Had God only formed this covenant with Abram, it could have easily expired upon his death. But God protected His everlasting covenant through Ishmael and a future birth to Sarai (90 years old) and Abram (100 years old); a son named Isaac.

The mark of circumcision, made by cutting away the foreskin, allowed the covenant to be a visible seal within the flesh. In return, God promises Abram that He will be his God and the God of his descendants—a unique relationship between God and man is born. You must admit one thing about good ole Abram—he was an astute follower. At least, that is, enough to accept the circumcision deal from God as stated without trying to negotiate out of the pain. Sometimes it seems we are much more bold than our predecessors as we attempt to strike deals with God when He asks a lot of us. A lesson from obedient Abram is a good thing to remember.

God changed Abram's name to Abraham in verse 5. We will talk more about this later . . . stay tuned.

Ponder for a moment this message from God to Abram (now Abraham). God chose a small and intimate group for circumcision so He could properly build up His people. He did not include everyone in the village or town. He did not advise them to circumcise every traveler who came by. He chose to build everything upon the stable foundation of Abraham. The intimate direction and instruction from God to His people would be essential to these earliest followers. God did, however, continue to grow His base throughout the Old Testament. For instance, it is interesting that in the book of Leviticus 23:42 when God directs the Israelites to celebrate a Feast of Booths, He includes only the native Israelites. Then, in the later chapter of Deuteronomy 16:14, He would add the community's Levite, alien, orphan and widow to the Feast of Booths invitation list. It was not until His only Son came to Earth that all of us would be included on the "salvation" invitation list. Halleluiah!

If circumcision was an old law pertaining to the covenant between God and the Jews in the Old Testament, then what is the significance of circumcision in the New Testament? Was it addressed in the writings of Christ's apostles and disciples? How can one law be so important in the Old Testament and not remain so in the New Testament? Does circumcision fall to the wayside because it is too difficult to enforce or is there a metamorphosis of sorts taking place within the new Christian community?

Although we did some work above as we uncovered the beginning of this covenant between Abraham and God, you may find it interesting to note that circumcision is discussed in many of the Old Testament books. Below is a review of the highlights:

- o   First, the law is established in Genesis.
- o   In Exodus, the law is specified again as a Passover Feast requirement, in that no man uncircumcised may partake in the festivities; however, foreigners living among the Israelites could participate as long as they "went under the knife" first. (Wow, that is quite a hefty cover charge!)
- o   Leviticus, a book containing the prescribed ritual laws of the tribe of Levi, also addresses who should be circumcised and when. Later in Leviticus, and again in Deuteronomy, "Circumcision of the Heart" begins to unfold. As the circumcised continue to defy and rebel against God, a new conversion is spoken of. It is not enough to merely "look" holy in the flesh, but it is the heart that must also be cut open (or humbled) for God to enter. Hardened hearts and closed minds were causing the people to fall away from God leaving them helpless and lost—not only "literally" in the desert, but also "spiritually" without God.
- o   In the book of Joshua, Moses' successor explains that God required the Israelites, upon arrival into the Promised Land, to

circumcise all of the boys born in the desert during the forty-year journey (since they had ceased mandating circumcision during the hardship).

o   In the books of Judges, 1 Samuel, 1 Chronicles, Isaiah, Jeremiah, and Ezekiel, the word "uncircumcised" is used to imply enemy. It is interesting that, in these books, the Israelites often refer to themselves as the "circumcised," not unlike we now call ourselves Catholics or Christians.

(For detail on the above scripture passages, refer to Genesis 17:10, Exodus 12:48, Leviticus 26:40-43, Deuteronomy 30:6, Joshua 5:7, Judges 15:18, 1 Samuel 17:36, 1 Chronicles 10:4, Isaiah 52:1, Jeremiah 9:24-25, Ezekiel 28:10.)

Let us now end the Old Testament segment with one last passage before we begin studying the New Testament. It serves as the perfect segue. Open your Bible to the prophetic book of Jeremiah 4:1-4.

God has a bit of advice to share with the wayward souls of Israel. He commands them to examine their spiritually barren lives (untilled ground) and to spring into action (till it). Yet he warns them not to do so while still living a sinful life (thorns). Even the best intentions for reconciling with God are lost if we continue our evil habits. Our Lord calls us to a new kind of circumcision, a circumcision of the heart. Allowing our hearts to harden destroys our relationship with God. Unlike the ritual of circumcision on the flesh, which is performed by one onto another, we are the ones in control of our own circumcised (or hardened) heart. God places the responsibility back on us.

Did you notice at the end of the fourth verse, God does GET ANGRY! His warning is clear and his patience is immense, but He will get angry. In fact, God's anger sits at the edge of dangerous waters warning us to turn away. It is only when we no longer hear His voice of protection and his roar of anger against evil that we will know the world has ended.

With the New Testament comes the Savior of the World to show us the way. Halleluiah, praise to God Almighty! Finally, the people have the

Savior in the flesh; teaching and leading them, living among them and then dying for them. Certainly that clears everything up and all people finally see and then follow the light of Christ, right? Wrong. Read Acts 7:51-52.

These verses capture the conclusion of a set of discourses in which Saint Stephen tried to help the closed-minded understand their errors as he encouraged them to turn back to God. The very wise and Spirit-filled Stephen speaks out to the Sanhedrin and to the high priest. Sadly, after this remarkable and honest warning, he is stoned to death.

Paul is the one who addresses the new law of circumcision in this next scripture passage. The question was whether or not the early Christians should all be the same—all circumcised or all uncircumcised. You can probably imagine the confusion as the melting pot of early Christians sought the truth and the will of God. Do they all need to be of one likeness as was dictated in the Old Testament? Paul clarifies in 1 Corinthians 7:17-20. Please read the scripture passage.

It is not circumcision that unites God's called people but rather the commandments of God. The rules of God will bind the disparate into a common flock. God uses commandments to discipline, contain and protect his sheep. He knows the closer we stay to the shepherd the clearer we can hear his warnings or calls for change in direction.

That, too, is why we must embrace the steadfast rules of the Catholic Church. They are set by God to keep us safe. Like a fence has many posts, the principles of Catholicism serve as timeless moral boundaries. Faith is the span of fencing stretched across the secure and deep catechismal pillars. Without posts a fence would fall. Without a fence the pillars stand untenable. Rules need faith and faith needs rules. Therefore, the strict dogma of the Catholic Church and the faith we place in upholding each principle is our best defense against the lurking and ever-hungry wolves.

In this next scripture passage, Galatians 6:14-15, Paul teaches us another lesson on the subject. Please read it now for further insight.

He addresses those who boast about a physical circumcision and yet forget the cross of Christ that saved them. How many times do we get so caught up in "belonging" that we forget our purpose? God works patiently and methodically, perfecting his creations over time, but we are the ones who must recognize where we are in the journey to holy perfection and how much work still needs to be done for His will.

We are asked to carry our cross and to live in the example of Christ so fully that Christ is the one working through us. We are asked to die of self and the sins that separate us from God, so that we may be born of the perfect Christ. It is a difficult task but it is our purpose and it is the most rewarding of all—to allow God's gifts to work within us for His Almighty Glory. To summarize the biblical transition from circumcision to new birth let's look to Paul again as he clarifies the "new creation."

> *So whoever is in Christ is a new creation: the old things have passed away; behold, new things have come. 2 Corinthians 5:17*

DISCUSSION CORNER

A farmer needs to till, seed, water, and harvest only to do the same tilling, seeding, watering and harvesting the next year, and the next. Discuss how the seasons of our life and faith resemble that of a farmer.

How do we know if we have achieved a "circumcised heart"? Why is it so difficult for us, as it was with the first Christians, to constantly maintain an open heart in a secular world?

Do you remember a time when the words of St. Paul (in the above scripture) especially came true for you? Think of the times when choosing Jesus over the world led to new things in your life. Share your thoughts with others in your group.

THE CUSTOM OF CIRCUMCISION

Have you ever wondered why Catholics baptize shortly after birth and some non-Catholic Christians wait until adulthood? Although there are many reasons, I think it is important to discuss the one that relates to this first chapter on circumcision. Catholics believe that Paul instructs us to look at Baptism as the metamorphosis of Circumcision in the Old Testament. He reveals to us that before Christ circumcision was a necessary rite to mark God's chosen people but that we are now circumcised through Christ. We are buried with Jesus through the plunging into the water of Baptism and we are raised with him through faith and God's forgiveness. Let's review the ancient custom of circumcision to discover for ourselves the transition to Baptism.

I was fortunate to be able to interview a man who would prove to be extremely helpful to me as I put this chapter together. Dr. Alan Bercovitz (note1-1) was able to shed light on Judaism's ritual of circumcision, point out the bridge to Catholicism and also add a bit of insight about the secular view of circumcision, which I had not even considered. Alan is a medical doctor who was raised in a devout Jewish home but who fell in love with and married a devout Catholic woman. Together they baptized and raised their children in the Catholic faith. Alan has embraced the blessings and wisdom that come through this unique set of life experiences. He deeply cherishes both religions and can identify the similarities and the differences. His comprehension of Catholic traditions is deepened, as he is able to connect them to God's ancient rituals and laws. The same rituals and customs that Jesus followed would morph through our Savior into the universal church of Catholicism. Some we recognize easily and others have grown dim with time. He is uniquely positioned to remind us of their importance and the reverence in which we should hold them.

Alan has been an honored participant in the Jewish ritual of Brit Milah, or Bris as it is commonly known. Brit Milah is Hebrew for "covenant of circumcision." When he spoke to me about this ritual he spoke with reverence. This day is considered sacred and is one, if not the only, ritual permitted to take place on a Jewish holiday. If the eighth day of the boy's life falls on a holy day the circumcision must not be moved. The only reason that a male child should not be circumcised on this day is if the child is too weak or ill to have the procedure done. In that case, another day would be chosen for him.

The ceremony itself is short in length, only taking about 15 minutes, and is usually conducted in the home of the child's parents. The ceremony has three distinct parts:

1. Blessings and Circumcision
2. Kiddush (blessings of the wine) and Naming
3. Seudat Mitzah (celebratory meal)

As the ceremony begins the mother hands the child to the Kvatterin who then enters into the room prepared for the circumcision. The child then is passed into the arms of the Kvatter. The Kvatter then rests him in the arms of the Sandek who will hold the baby boy during the shedding of blood as the instrument held by the Mohel instigates the circumcision along with special prayers and blessings.

The blessing of the wine follows which is given in droplets to soothe the child immediately afterward. Next comes the very important part of naming the child. Once the child's name is announced, more prayers follow and the child is blessed and consecrated to God. Beautiful prayers both honor God as our Creator and King of the Universe and ask for mercy upon the child. Gifts of humility are requested during the naming portion of the ceremony, such as gifts of a pure heart and wisdom of God's laws.

It was the naming part of the ceremony that carried me back over 2000 years to the dwelling place where Joseph and Mary consecrated Jesus to God through this Jewish ritual. Oh how God did allow the fullness of all gifts to pour forth upon his only begotten son, Jesus, as he would grow to most fully comprehend the holy Law and he would teach it in the synagogues. Jesus would come to not only fulfill his Father's laws but to perfect them, establishing a New Covenant and the new law of Christianity—through his teaching, beatitudes, parables, and a command to love God with all our heart and to love one another.

Heaven would have rejoiced as their Prince of Peace was announced on earth and consecrated to Heaven. Once spoken, the precious name of Jesus would trumpet through the humble dwelling walls to the angels above. With holy echoes it would rise to the heavens that brightened with anticipation until it softly rested at the mighty throne of the loving and proud Father who sent him to save the world He loved.

At the conclusion of the ritual family and friends all celebrate a meal to mark the happy and sacred occasion of bringing another child into the covenant of Abraham, which is commanded by and pleasing to God.

Three things struck me as he walked me through the ceremony: The names of the supporting adults chosen by the parents for the child, the ritual process and the blessings that are recited. I thought, *this ceremony sounds very familiar.* This ritual closely resembles the Catholic Sacrament of Baptism. Let's take a closer look as we compare each ritual:

o   Translated, the words Kvatterin and Kvatter mean godmother and godfather, respectively. Catholic parents, with great care, choose a godmother and godfather that will stand beside and support the child throughout his life. In both ceremonies, these roles are considered honorable.

o   In both traditions the newly born child of God is the focal point of thanksgiving, petition, and sacrificial honor as it both welcomes into and requests protection through God's covenant.

o   Both rituals use the baby's name as an important part of the prayer.

o   The Jewish prayers consecrate the baby into the religion of Judaism through which he will serve God as he grows and matures in faith. The Catholic prayers consecrate the baby into the religion of Catholicism through which he will serve God as he grows and matures in faith.

o   Both rituals share a similar cadence as they begin with blessings, call for an action (circumcision or baptism) that is consistent with the teaching and then end with a meal of celebration.

o   No blood is shed in a baptism because we have been saved through the blood of Christ, and that baptism is the "circumcision of Christ". In baptism we are called both to die of sin and to be reborn or resurrected with Christ through the waters of baptism. As Paul would call us, "a new creation".

According to Paul's letter to the Colossians below, this is the example Catholics follow and is one reason Catholics justify the need for infant baptism just as God required circumcision of the eight day old child:

> *For in him dwells the whole fullness of the deity bodily, and you share in this fullness in him, who is the head of every principality and power. In him you were also circumcised with a circumcision not administered by hand, by stripping off the carnal body, with the circumcision of Christ. You were buried with him in baptism, in which you were also raised with him through faith in the power of God, who raised him from the dead. Colossians 2:9-12*

The last thing that I will leave you with on the lesson of this custom is what Dr. Bercovitz shared with me about clinical circumcisions within our secular society. As a physician he has both observed and performed circumcisions on newborn infants before they leave the hospital. After attending ceremonies of both Bris and Baptism he recalls that even this commonplace surgical procedure, performed in a sterile atmosphere within a secular society, cannot be considered ordinary. As he spoke I could hear the reverence for circumcision that has not been lost on him. I could also detect his intense gratefulness and awe for God's newly born creations. It was a great reminder to me that, tradition or not, our awe and reverence are always well placed in our Creator God.

DISCUSSION CORNER

Discuss the timing of your own baptism and memories from baptisms you have witnessed over your life. Include times you may have selected or participated as a godparent. Looking back, what stands out to you now that may have been overlooked before studying these scripture passages?

THE IMPORTANCE OF NAMES

Now we get to study names for a while! Earlier in this chapter we found in scripture that God chose to change Abram's name to Abraham because he was going to make him *"the father of a host of nations"*. Abram means "High Father" in Hebrew, yet Abraham translates to "Father of Many". Now it is true that God can do whatever He wants, so He could have chosen to allow Abram to stay with the name he had grown accustomed to hearing—for the past ninety-nine years! Why the imposition of changing the name of a man to fit a newly created job assignment? Why did God choose to complicate things for this faithful man?

God wanted every detail to be perfect and to be marked appropriately for this historical occasion of a new and everlasting covenant between God and Man. God assigns names, He uses them as a mold to shape and transform us, and He wants each name to fit the person He created. So, was it just Abram that received the name change, or were there others? And what about the times in Scripture where God dictated a name before the babies even entered the womb? All I can think is: names must be VERY IMPORTANT to God.

Find below some Scriptural confirmation. Let's check it out and play a few name games. Read along with the provided Bible passages and the name definitions taken from the website Behindthename.com. (note 1-2)

1. ISHMAEL m Biblical

From the Hebrew name יִשְׁמָעֵאל *(Yishma'el)* meaning "God will hear"

Abram and Sarai's marriage had not been blessed with children. Wanting to experience motherhood, Sarai thought it was a good idea to request that her husband lay with her maidservant, Hagar, that she might become pregnant. Warning! Be careful what you ask for—or in this case, demand! Hagar, as instructed, became pregnant and an illegitimate son was to be born. Hagar beamed, Sarai balked, and Abram backpedaled as the resentment of the newest pregnancy in the household escalated. At one very desperate point Hagar pleaded in prayer and it was to her that these words were spoken:

> *Then the LORD's angel said to her:*
> *"You are now pregnant and shall bear a son;*
> *you shall name him Ishmael,*
> *For the LORD has heeded your affliction. Genesis 16:11*

Hagar and Abram's son was to be called Ishmael. Look at the above Hebrew meaning. This is exactly what God did for Hagar, his mother.

A few years after Ishmael's birth things again got rocky around the homestead and Hagar and Ishmael were banished to the desert. Without food or water the mother and child were reaching certain death until, once again, God heard the cries of the young Ishmael. God sent a messenger to comfort and provide for them.

> *God heard the boy's voice, and God's angel called to Hagar from heaven: "What is the matter, Hagar? Do not fear; God has heard the boy's voice in this plight of his." Genesis 21:17*

2. SARAI f Biblical

Possibly means "contentious" in Hebrew

SARAH f English, French, German, Hebrew, Arabic, Biblical, Biblical Hebrew
Means "lady" or "princess" in Hebrew

Please follow along through Genesis 17:15-20. In verse 15 Abraham's wife Sarai was to be changed to Sarah. (Now this one will make you chuckle.) Sarai in Hebrew is thought to have meant contentious, but Sarah, in Hebrew, means lady or princess. What a sense of humor God does have! Only He could change an "argumentative wife" into a "princess" worthy of the gifts He was about to unleash. She became a 90-year-old pregnant woman who would deliver a God-fearing son. Only God, only God!

3. ISAAC m English, Hebrew (Anglicized), Biblical, Biblical Latin

From the Hebrew name יִצְחָק *(Yitzchaq)* which meant "he laughs"

Staying with the same scripture as above, notice verse 19 where Abraham and Sarah's child shall be called Isaac. Isaac means "he laughs". What did Abraham do in verse 17 while prostrating himself to God?

Please read Genesis 18:12-15 for another excerpt that provides further insight about Sarah's reaction to her very late-in-life pregnancy.

Yes, Sarah did laugh when she overheard the news. Wouldn't you? Please look again at the great question stated in verse 14. In my Bible, I have underlined and starred it in red so I might never forget it. I call upon its omnipotence when I feel overwhelmed for truly there is **nothing** too marvelous for God to do. Abraham, like us, already knew the answer to the question but needed to be reminded of our Lord God's unlimited power and might. Yes, even though Sarah denied it at first, she did indeed laugh! At their ages, I believe God had the last laugh on this miracle.

4. JOHN m English, Biblical

English form of *Iohannes*, the Latin form of the Greek name *Ιωαννης (Ioannes)*, itself derived from the Hebrew name יוחנן *(Yochanan)* meaning "YAHWEH is gracious".

> *But the angel said to him, "Do not be afraid, Zechariah, because your prayer has been heard. Your wife Elizabeth will bear you a son, and you shall name him John. And you will have joy and gladness, and many will rejoice at his birth, for he will be great in the sight of [the] Lord. He will drink neither wine nor strong drink. He will be filled with the holy Spirit even from his mother's womb, and he will turn many of the children of Israel to the Lord their God. Luke 1:13-15*

Zechariah is John the Baptist's father. Once again, God sends an angel to deliver His name of choice to an expectant parent. Look again at what John in Hebrew means. Verse 15 states that the child will be "filled with the Holy Spirit" even within the womb of his mother.

Interesting side note: Do you recall in scripture that, immediately after saying yes to the angel of God, Mary visited her relative Elizabeth? The infant in Elizabeth's womb, John the Baptist, actually *"leaped in her womb"* upon first hearing the voice belonging to the mother of his Savior,

Jesus. This unborn child was indeed "filled with the Holy Spirit" as was prophesized and fulfilled within Scripture.

The meaning of his name gives us some idea about the possible approach John the Baptist took as he called to the children of Israel to return to their God (Yahweh). John would be blessed with, and have wisdom of, the gracious gifts of the Lord their God. To an oppressed Jewish nation these would be words of profound encouragement and renewed faith. Even though many had turned from God, He had not abandoned them.

What God had planned was more than Zechariah could have imagined. John was to be more than a prophet for the people of Israel; he would come to not only gather but to cleanse the "first" children of God through the waters of baptism. He would demand repentance and call for change. He would preach in earnest and with haste for the assignment he was given: to prepare the way for the Savior of the world, Jesus Christ. And furthermore, John the Baptist would have the privilege and honor of baptizing Jesus in the Jordan River! (cf. Matthew 3:13-17)

John the Baptist has an amazing story behind his name, but we can just cover a few high points today. When you have the time, read the rest of Luke 1: 5-25 and 57-80 to fully understand or reacquaint yourself with the story of his conception, naming, and birth before he began his ministry to announce our Lord Jesus. It truly is a fascinating narrative of disbelief, prophecy, obedience, and thanksgiving.

THE NAME ABOVE ALL NAMES

It began most humbly when God sent the angel Gabriel to Mary to announce the coming of Our Savior and to establish his name as Jesus. But it was not until his circumcision that he would formally be given the name, as is the Jewish custom. The naming and the circumcision of an eight-day-old male child was previously set up by God and remained a sacred ceremony, especially for the Son of God.

Oh! how the heavens must have rejoiced as the name, above all names, was proclaimed by Joseph and Mary. It is wondrous to imagine the moment in which they were asked to profess the child's name. In that instant when Joseph looked at Mary, and Mary at Joseph, they understood the Higher Power behind this name. What may have seemed mere seconds in earthly time was no doubt an eternity in heaven as they waited in anticipation for the Prince of Peace to claim his name. And so, with united and obedient hearts, the mother and father declared for their son the name above all names. It was now official. The wondrous name that was created and chosen by God, revealed in trust to the angel Gabriel, announced to Mary and fortified through a dream to Joseph, would eventually establish a divide for the remainder of time. So important a name it would mark the end of B.C. years and bring forth a new calendar of hope. Anticipated for generations, revered by those who walked the earth beside him, and forever murmured by his faithful followers, the name of Jesus would change the world forever.

I will make your name renowned through all generations;
thus nations shall praise you forever. Psalm 45:18

Read the Catholic Link below, taken directly from the *Catechism of the Catholic Church*, for a beautiful synopsis of "the name" which reins above all names and for all names.

Catholic Link

Catechism of the Catholic Church

2666 But the one name that contains everything is the one that the Son of God received in his incarnation: JESUS. The divine name may not be spoken by human lips, but by assuming our humanity The Word of God hands it over to us and we can invoke it: "Jesus," "YHWH saves."[16]

The name "Jesus" contains all: God and man and the whole economy of creation and salvation. To pray "Jesus" is to invoke him and to call him within us. His name is the only one that contains the presence it signifies. Jesus is the Risen One, and whoever invokes the name of Jesus is welcoming the Son of God who loved him and who gave himself up for him.[17]

[16] Cf. *Ex* 3:14; 33:19-23; *Mt* 1:21. [17] *Rom* 10:13; *Acts* 2:21; 3:15-16; *Gal* 2:20.

The Catholic link above reminds us that when we call out his name, we are inviting him into our hearts. This paragraph should also cause us to reflect on any times we have misused or silently witnessed as others have flippantly used his holy name.

When we study the importance that God has placed on names and if we acknowledge how it feels to have our own name abused or misused, we can then imagine what God and Jesus have endured over the centuries. The unequivocal respect that should be granted to God is not always the way of the world. In fact, given the abuse and misuse tagged to their holy names, it is a wonder that we still stand. Would you not, if you had a God-powered magic wand, cast down those who repeatedly abused your name or your precious child's name? You would think that we would be more sensitive to it, but we hear God and Jesus' names irreverently used often in our workplaces, social settings, movies and television shows. Maybe we should be more appalled when we hear it and voice our concern. Maybe we should pay closer attention to something that is so important to our God.

> *Tell the Israelites: Anyone who blasphemes God shall bear the penalty; whoever utters the name of the LORD in a curse shall be put to death. The whole community shall stone that person; alien and native-born alike must be put to death for uttering the LORD's name in a curse.*
>
> *Leviticus 24:15-16*

And if that was not enough he even wrote it on a stone tablet, placing it in His very own "Top 10 List". Perhaps God's patience grows thinner each day the number who "say" His name outweighs the number who "pray" His name. We do not realize what little changes we can make to bring Him joy.

YOUR NAME

What is your name? With intention whisper it or think it right now. Did you choose your full given name, a shortened version, or a nickname? If asked to write it would you have chosen a more formal name, like your signature, or something more casual?

As for my name, when I am writing to my family or close friends, I simply sign my name as "B". It is who I have become to many of my nieces and nephews who call me Aunt B. I love the simplicity and the affinity in which they bestowed this nickname upon me, so it has stuck. Some of my dearest adult friends call me Bethy, a nickname I had not heard spoken since I was very young. To me it seems smoother off the tongue, the difference between a sturdy four-legged kitchen chair and the comfort of grandma's rocker. Maybe that is why they like it.

I wonder if God calls me B, Beth, or Bethy when He refers to me or asks one of His angels to check on me. You know He talks about us because He created, knows and loves us. He even answers our prayers, so what *does* He call us? Do we have a heavenly name all our own—as unique to us as our fingerprint? Or is it so confusing that He just points to us to say what He wants to say? I don't think so, because names are so important to Him. He calls us something and I'll bet it is beautiful.

Have you ever noticed how your own name sounds different and stirs different emotions within you depending on who is saying it and with what purpose? You may recall the sweetness of your name as it left the mouth of many loved ones and even how it sounded on their caring lips. We love hearing our names that way. We can also recall the bitterness of it on the tongue of others. Maybe they were making fun of our name or us. Perhaps it was simply someone we surmised had evil intentions and we did not think that our name was safe in their mouth; in fact, we did not want them to know it or to say it. It is times like this we want to guard our name and protect it as if it were something they could steal from us, yet it is only a name. Or is our name really more than that?

Assignment: Write down all your given names (include first, middle, confirmation, and any nicknames) then go to a website (i.e., behindthename. com) or any book that lists names and their meanings. Look up any or all names associated with you. Write any significant details pertaining to your names.

Discuss what you found in researching your name. Did you learn anything new about yourself? Does your name fit you? Is there a nickname that may better fit your characteristics?

Think about whether you developed into your name over time, if it always has described you to a tee, or if you possibly lost what once defined you. Is your name a secret clue to the inner being yet to be tapped into?

BAPTISMAL NAMES

Some churches choose to hold baptism services privately before or after Mass but our parish chooses to perform them during our Saturday evening or Sunday Masses. I really appreciate the beauty and essence of this sacrament and that all parishioners are asked to participate in the Christian growth and faith of our newest member. Our entire congregation is invited to participate in renewing our baptismal promises and restating our rejection of Satan. It is a cleansing experience.

According to the *Catechism of the Catholic Church (#2156)*, the Christian name given to us at Baptism signifies our name in the Church. This name, if chosen from Christian names preceding us, unites our name to our "patron saint." A name may also link to a "Christian mystery" or to a "Christian virtue". This patron saint, mystery or virtue will provide us with an important model of charity and will intercede for us. As I watch the Catholic infant baptisms I have to wonder whom else may be present, not unlike the host of angels that were present at our Savior's birth. Certainly this newest child from God, consecrated back to Him for his days on Earth, does not go unnoticed or uncelebrated by those in Heaven.

THE LESSON

As I studied and meditated on this first time Jesus shed blood for us I had to wonder about the pain and suffering that goes along with having your flesh cut into. But I had to surmise that Jesus would not have us focus on this suffering alone. Many scholars believe that Jesus, because of his divine nature, always has felt and always will feel our suffering and pain. We know this is true with God. Human infants, however, do not understand someone else's pain and suffering until they are older. Since Jesus was both divine and human, we do not know when he acquired this knowledge as man. If like all other human beings, Jesus was not born with this understanding, when did he begin suffering for us?

Since God loves to mark special occasions in spectacular fashion, do you think the circumcision of Jesus may also have opened up his pure and stainless heart to know our sufferings and pain? The first drops of his precious blood were shed for our salvation during this occasion, commencing an everlasting flow of payment for our sinful debt.

Perhaps Jesus knew all from the womb, but perhaps this ceremony would mark the occasion in which the new covenant would be revealed and a most perfect "Circumcision of the Heart" would take place. That would mean that Jesus did, at only eight days of age, have clear understanding of our needs, desires, sufferings, sorrows and pain. He would have felt them, understood them, and embraced them, as he grew in wisdom and in favor of God, his Father.

Of course, we have no way of knowing for sure the exact moment Jesus (as man) knew he would be called to die for us, but we do know his blood was valued greater than all of our sins combined. When our wondering leads us back to His great love and to His words within Holy Scripture for answers, then it is doing what it is supposed to do. Maybe that is why the Bible will never be outdated and will continue to captivate all who study it. Our faith will be sufficient until God reveals all.

CLOSING PRAYER

Dear Lord,

We love You and praise You. Thank You for Your precious Son, Jesus, who teaches us about his circumcision and naming. As we meditate on the first blood that was shed from the earthly body of Christ, we know that without it we would not be saved. We thank You for loving us. We thank You for desiring our presence in eternity, so much that You sacrificed Your son in payment for our offenses.

We ask that we may never become so callused to Your name, or that of Your Son, that we do not protect them and keep them sacred. Also, that we may learn from this lesson of blood and suffering that our hearts must be open to Your Word and that our earthly desires must die so that we may live in You. Teach us, dear Lord, as our eyes are open to these wounds, what You desire for us to know. Guide us, dear Lord, that Your will may be done through us. Accept and use our circumcised hearts for Your glory. Amen.

First Prayer: The Circumcision

The Prayer of St. Bridget for The Circumcision

Pray 1 Our Father, 1 Hail Mary, then:

Eternal Father, through Mary's unblemished hands and the Divine Heart of Jesus, I offer You the first wounds, the first pains, and the first Bloodshed as atonement for my and all of humanity's sins of youth, as protection against the first mortal sin, especially among my relatives.

The Suffering on the Mount of Olives (Agony in the Garden)

Bible passages needed for study of this chapter:

Luke 22:39-46	John 15:20-27	Mark 14:36
John 14:29-30	Luke 4:1-13	Mark 14:37-41
John 12:27-28	Revelation 3:15-17	
John 12:23-26	Matthew 26: 39	

For the Agony in the Garden, please read Luke 22:39-46.

We begin our study with this scripture because Luke's gospel is the only one that goes into the detail of Christ's extreme agony and fervent prayer.

In verse 44, his sweat was like drops of blood, which fell upon the ground. Again, this reveals a time when Jesus' precious and sacred blood was being shed for our salvation. This time, however, it would not be from a wound or cut, but rather from an extreme internal turmoil and anxiety that would push out the droplets of blood from his wracked and sweating body. In this final hour before his arrest, conflict would emerge as his will struggled against the inherent vulnerabilities of his humanness.

To me, there is no greater biblical description for us to realize how truly human our Savior was than "The Agony in the Garden." He survived, on this night, more anguish than any man could imagine. God will never again require one man's brutal death in exchange for the sins of the world. That job was reserved for the only man who could comprehend, embrace and accomplish it . . . and even the only begotten Son of God struggled with its weight. During his prayer, he would exercise his free will to question and fervently petition his Father in Heaven for a way of escaping what was closing in on him. Yet he would respectfully yield to the will of God as he held tight to the promise he came to fulfill.

CLINICALLY SPEAKING

Why did Luke mention the droplets of blood mixed with sweat in his gospel while the others left it out? To add only more confusion, it was discovered that Luke's original writings did not include this part of the suffering; it was added to his gospel at some point after his original manuscripts were widely dispersed. Could it be because it was noticed by the disciples and apostles that night but not understood, so therefore it was considered an obscure and inconsequential detail?

Since Luke was not present himself, his account of the gospel was based on investigating and compiling events from eyewitnesses. Luke was the beloved physician (Col. 4:14) in the bunch, so his training may have directed him to ponder what others told him of the abnormal physical condition of Jesus. Maybe he wrote about it, then could not diagnose it, and therefore deleted it. Perhaps he did not write it but queried other physicians about it until word of mouth landed on someone who understood its significance and had it added to the gospel. Possibly it is a miracle: a person who was led by God to find the missing piece of history and correct His Book.

However it got there, the two verses (43 and 44) did appear and will forever document the truth of the final hours of Christ Jesus.

It is difficult for us to imagine this type of extreme anxiety because so few people have ever experienced it. This rare medical condition is known as hematidrosis (note 2-1) and is considered a physiological phenomenon. As I understand it, it begins in a copious sweat brought on when the body, mind or spirit is placed under pressure. However, when the most extreme conditions occur, the body can actually break open blood capillaries, resulting in droplets of blood being pushed out and mixing with the human sweat. (note 2-2)

In addition, this type of affliction leaves the body more vulnerable and more sensitive to pain. (note2-3) Jesus' body had no time to repair itself before the flogging and crucifixion and therefore this Agony in the Garden of Gethsemane added even more suffering to what he endured throughout his brutal arrest, scourging, crowning and crucifixion. And every drop of blood was credited to our sinful debt and continued until it was paid in full, that we might share eternal life with God. Amazing!

A CUSTOM OF PRAYER

Staying with the above verses from Luke, let's look at verse 39 again. This passage leads us to believe that this was not the first time Jesus took the disciples to this garden for prayer. It seems from these words, and from other gospels, that Jesus was accustomed to retreating here for prayer. No doubt, this was not the only city in which Jesus kept this custom. In fact chances are good that no matter where he was—in a small town or rocking city, in a fishing boat upon the sea or climbing a mountain, in a sweltering desert or pitching tent on the cool forest floor, in a house full of tax collectors or a home among extended family—he would always seek, and then find, a comfortable and quiet place to be alone with his Father.

Do we follow Jesus' example? Do we seek that place that soothes us and in return gives glory to God? Do we frequent it only at home or do we find it when we are working away from home, visiting a friend, or fortunate enough to take a vacation? Is it always a priority for us, a custom if you will, to find this place for prayer?

Perhaps without even realizing it, biblical authors would write about one experience and through it would reveal so many other traits and characteristics of Jesus. They may have thought his routine trivial, as it became a familiar practice for them, yet these insightful passages provide inspiration to each of us while exposing the very disciplined life he led. They serve as examples we can use to understand how Jesus made it through the tough times and how he stayed on mission and task.

He was divine but also human. He got tired, just like we do. He had sorrows, just like we do. He had questions, just like we do. He needed help staying on track, just like we do. He sought and found refuge, just like . . . DO WE? If Jesus relied on it and taught it to his disciples, what makes us think we do not also need prayer?

Our world runs at a fast and furious pace. Think of His love, mercy and guidance as individual broadcasts sent repeatedly via the heavenly airways. Where is your antenna? Is it buried somewhere in the back yard or carried with you at all times? Are you picking up the right signal or is your antenna locked on a 24-hour sports, food, or gossip channel?

Like a cell phone with tentative reception, we must intentionally seek or create the best places for clear reception. You may recall some of your own past cell phone experiences when continuous and uninterrupted service was at a premium. Did you ever have to contort like a gymnast and then freeze in position just to finish a conversation? Or were you driving and had to pull off the road because you knew you were approaching another dreaded dead zone. Were those conversations any more important than the conversation God is trying to have with each of us? Do we go to such extremes to hear Him?

Please take time to think about, and then discuss with others, your victories of prayer (when you make it to "the garden") and when you are most vulnerable to fall off track (when your "tuner" is not receiving). Include the conditions that are most inviting for you to converse with God through prayer and those in which it is nearly impossible. Share ideas with each other of how to fortify good habits for prayer.

Engaging in the custom of prayer rewarded Jesus, gave great glory to God, and saved all of mankind. (Not too bad for a poor carpenter's son!) Can you think of a way that God could help you more or use you more if you fully submitted to this custom?

A LOOK INSIDE THE MAN

Scripture portrays Jesus' temperament as normally calm, cool and collected. He was an inspiration to those who knew him and to the fortunate souls who heard him speak. Jesus spent much of his social time teaching or healing. He spoke openly to his disciples about his purpose on Earth, the impending sacrifice of his life and even how he was to die (Mark 8:31-32). It causes us to question why a man, so fully engaged and aware of the plan for his death, should so anxiously sweat under its weight. Why did Jesus ask for the cup to be taken away from him? What provoked his earnest request?

His motive was not instigated by self-pity or remorse. Jesus had not sinned so he had no regrets to confess as we would if put in this same situation. Jesus was squared away with His Father and actually looked forward to being with Him once again in Heaven. Would Jesus' only concern be for us? It leads us to wonder what was behind all the anxiousness of this night. Let us look to scripture to see what we can gather about the final hours of Our Savior.

To put it in perspective, on the evening of the Agony in the Garden, Jesus is in requisite mode. He has less than twenty-four hours before he is to leave this world and only a few hours to teach them how to survive without him. The disciples would soon scatter from fear so it was crucial that his words be spoken with purpose and conviction, leaving them a solid thread of hope to cling to. They would constantly replay the final words of Christ, trying to recall the painful words they previously wished to dismiss. Jesus would need to warn them of this world and encourage them about the next. What he would ask of them would not be easy. He would return as the risen Christ but that would not be for days, so for the frightened and hunted it would seem like . . . an eternity.

Of course, the disciples had memories to hold on to. After all—he was teacher extraordinaire, performed miracles beyond belief, touched their hearts, rebuked their lack of faith and gave all glory to His Father in Heaven. He was amazing and they loved him greatly and followed him faithfully. But the teacher was leaving and the final exam had been prepared. How would you grade his followers? Let's see . . . . Well, not a single one stayed awake with him in the Garden. Of the twelve in his inside circle, one will be paid off to betray him, most will flee to safety when he is arrested, and his beloved follower will deny him not once, but three times. One might easily conclude that they don't get it; better to drop the class now and sign up for it again next semester. But the master will no longer be here and these men are the chosen teachers to carry the new covenant forward! Are you feeling a little twinge of anxiousness for Jesus about now?

To further complicate things, Jesus is leaving them in troubled waters, with hostile people who are committed to ending any spread of what would later become Christianity. Jesus will be returning to his Father, the Ruler of Heaven, but they are to remain on Earth with another ruler. Read John 14:29-30.

Jesus speaks of the ruler of the world as Satan. Oh, that is not good, not good at all. Satan will seize this opportunity with gusto. As soon as the perfect shield falls, the poison arrows will be in flight. Satan will be ready to pounce as soon as Jesus leaves. Jesus knows this. Are his followers brave enough to carry the message forward?

Jesus speaks again in John 12:27-28. Please read that passage now.

Jesus admits that he is troubled as the hour approaches yet he remains steadfast. Listen as Jesus teaches the disciples about why he must die as you read another passage in John, just above the lines you just read. Please read John12: 23-26 for another important lesson on life and death.

After reading it we can better understand why Jesus had to die; we also get a glimpse of the life he called his apostles to. The growth of his church would either flourish or die in the hearts of those who knew him. Self-serving cowards with hardened hearts would smother it, while selfless warriors with open hearts would proliferate it. Two thousand years later we can marvel at its vastness, but it all had to start from a single grain planted by God into the hearts he trusted to carry it on.

Jesus continues to mix the hard talks with the words of encouragement:

> *"I have told you this so that you might have peace in me. In the world you will have trouble, but take courage, I have conquered the world." John 16:33*

Jesus warns his disciples again in this next scripture passage. Please read John 15:20-27.

These are heavy words falling on novice ears. Just days earlier his disciples witnessed Jesus being revered with palm branches as he strode into Jerusalem on a donkey. Now the world hates him? Impossible for them to understand yet it happened just as Jesus had foretold. In verses 20 and 21, Jesus speaks about himself as their master and about the predicament he leaves them with.

DISCUSSION CORNER

In verses 20 and 21 (above), it sounds like experiencing a secular persecution is a sign we are submitting to the correct master. Think about the hardships of serving God in this world. Discuss some persecutions that we should accept with honor because they are used to glorify God.

For every courageous godly action, Satan has a spin. What spin have you been tempted to trust before you came to your senses?

WORLDS APART

> *"If the world hates you, realize that it hated me first. If you belonged to the world, the world would love its own; but because you do not belong to the world, and I have chosen you out of the world, the world hates you." John 15:18-19*

Does being hated in this life mean that you should act grumpy or woeful? Certainly not, and Jesus did not. Does it mean that your life will be empty or shallow? No, actually it is quite the contrary. Jesus asks us to rely on God for everything because our happiness must come from Him (Matthew 6:25-33). Worldly happiness is dangerous to His children because it comes with deceitful strings attached. Satan destroys. God lifts us up. Satan is self-serving, while God offers us the pathway to eternal happiness and an imperishable inheritance (1 Peter 1:4).

Before we continue, let's reacquaint ourselves with Jesus being tempted in the desert by Satan. Please open to Luke 4:1-13 to read the exchange.

This passage is like the classic television game show. Satan, the wicked host, tries to make deals to lure the contestant, Jesus. Leveraging his physical fatigue after a forty-day fast in the desert, Satan approaches the man with his best offer in hand. To gauge his temperature, Satan begins with a little small talk and a non-threatening request. Jesus is courteous enough to answer, but won't play along. Satan tries harder to tempt him. Satan boasts of the grand prizes he has to offer . . . power, glory, and ownership. You have to admit, it is an impressive package of loot. Others would sell their souls for an offer this good; in fact, that is the very price Satan requires for his handsome proposition.

All Jesus has to do is bow down to Satan and the grand prize is his. The audience erupts; some are cheering the host's audacity while others boo him. As a relentless heckle threatens to whirl the show into a new direction, the host quickly reclaims the control by quoting scripture. A hush comes over the crowd. All eyes are on the contestant. It is Jesus who delivers the final and undisputed scripture passage that counters and trumps all others, thereby forcing an unscheduled commercial break because the game show host suddenly left the building—for a while at least.

Jesus denies the devil a single victory. How often do we fall for the small talk, only to be led deeper into the abyss? (Note to self: Don't go into a desert without Jesus.)

It's a bit unsettling to know how cleverly Satan quotes scripture. It is true that he has been given many "things" of this world, which he uses to attract us to him. His attempts to ensnare God's chosen ones will work best on those who believe this life is all there is. If there is no God, no heaven, and no eternal dwelling place, then Satan is not a bad way to go. At least we can be happy for a little while, right? But what if that strategy is flawed? What if the Bible, the saints, the holy church, and all the miracles throughout the years prove to be spot on? What if God does exist and his promises are true? The inheritance will fall to the faithful and the patient. I WANT TO BE ONE OF THOSE! But the way of God is not so easy.

As soon as God blessed us with free will, He allowed us to choose Satan over Him. The decision is ours, and some do choose Satan. Jesus and Satan spoke the same language and could see things that humans cannot. Like the tempting in the desert, Satan would be front and forward in the Garden of Gethsemane; returning stronger and wiser than before the long commercial break. He would taunt his weakened victim once again, but this time with charm as he promised him the world. By taking out Jesus he would take out all of us, and what a victory that would be.

Scripture (Matthew 6:24) is clear that we can serve only one master. Which one do you trust will be around for eternity? Which one do you believe has your best interest at heart? This life is tough and even rotten at times but we can overcome it with God. Without God, we are as happy now as we will ever get. With God, well, there is so much more.

A verse that I committed to memory as a teenager has carried me through some tough times in my life. We can get through anything if we know it is a temporary dwelling place and that God's kingdom awaits us. This is what I memorized: *"What no man ever saw or heard, what no man ever thought could happen, are THE VERY THINGS that God has planned for those who love Him."* (cf 1 Corinthians 2:9, emphasis added)

This verse tells us we can try to imagine how wonderful God's kingdom is, but we cannot imagine it because it is not in our terms of happiness on earth. Jesus spoke of it from the cross as "Paradise" (Luke23:43).

Sometimes when I am really down, I play a little game of "Guess what heaven is like." I try to think of the most outrageous thing I can think of, leaving out no small detail. Sometimes the game goes on for a while as I push my mind to new heights, imagining what I would consider completely "over the top" or utterly impossible. And then I just say to myself with new conviction and a refreshed outlook: "No, it is even better than that."

As our measuring sticks of this world are obliterated, we will then feast our souls on a new and glorious set of standards. Nothing our little minds can muster will even be on the agenda. There will be far more beauty than our eyes have ever seen. The sound will be nothing we have ever heard. Things will happen that we thought impossible, but that will be just the start. Things we never knew could happen, not just miracles, but things we never knew existed will be our eternal norm.

Jesus eagerly awaited his disciples as he awaits us to join him in heaven, but for each of us on earth there is still much work to do. Jesus needed the apostles to carry out the mission after his death and resurrection. Come to think of it, Jesus still needs us to carry out his mission. If the apostles could hang on long enough to see it through, can't we too?

AGONY IN THE GARDEN

So, now let's go back to the garden scene. After Jesus speaks many words of warning and of strength in his final hours with the apostles, he enters the garden to pray. Jesus thinks of his apostles, one by one, and prays for them. But Jesus did not only die for them, he died for all mankind. So we need to broaden our telescope to bring in the entire world of past, present and future people. As we meditate on Jesus' agony, think of Satan's role in this night. Oh, how he would have loved to convince Jesus to turn from God in this hour. Scripture does not speak of Satan at this moment but we know he was there. Satan does not miss an opportunity like this one, and probably had more to do with Jesus' anxiety than we would like to give him credit for.

If we were to place ourselves in Satan's sandals on this night we would have to say, on the surface, that the cons for Jesus drinking the cup far outweigh the pros. Look at mankind. Look at the materialism, selfishness, drug abuse, abortions, sex predators, pornography, killing, greed, dishonesty, and the list goes on without stopping. We have taken goodness and made it evil. We have stripped God from our country's fiber and allowed Satan to weave his web of imprisonment. God forgives every infraction; Satan holds us captive to them.

We have settled for mediocrity and remained silent when we knew things were turning bad. Satan would use these things to remind Jesus that mankind is pitiful and that, given enough time, we will destroy ourselves. Really, why die for these people, Jesus? They are hopeless. Jesus would inevitably be reminded of those poor souls who would indeed turn their faces from God and fall deeper into the darkness. Jesus would pray fervently for the desperate souls most in need of his gracious mercy.

Like trying to outrace the rushing waterfalls with a sinking boat and a single oar, His energy would be spent and he would anxiously search for someone who would ease his mind. Mary, his blessed mother, would have filled that gap. Even if just for her, it would be worth the pain and suffering. But more beloved saints would enter the picture and from this Jesus would gain strength. The converts, the self-denying and the righteous would soothe his troubles. He would think of the worst sinners who turned their lives to God and, in doing so, would light the path for others. He would remember that God is willing to use every decision we make for His glory if we choose Him. He would possibly even smile a bit as he thought of those who would be most pleasing to His Father . . . until he remembered the last group.

Please read Revelation 3:15-17.

John writes candidly about the penalty reserved for the lukewarm. Look at the characteristics of the lukewarm in verse 17, first identifying how we see ourselves followed by what we truly look like to God. How can our perception be so far from reality? Blinded by comforts of this earth, we can remain in a state of lukewarm words, actions, and thoughts. To those, the Spirit of God speaks with an urgent awakening, calling us to repentance.

Here is one last thought regarding the anxiety that faced our Savior on that night; this has haunted me since the first time I meditated on the Agony in the Garden. I think about the people who must have pierced his heart with disgust and the people who revived it with hope. Then I learned about the lukewarm, and I shuddered.

If God would have randomly chosen only one picture to show Jesus that night, and it would have been mine, would Jesus have thought it worth all the pain and suffering he was asked to endure? I can only sigh.

Without a doubt, there are times Jesus would have run to the cross for me, and then times when I incessantly tried to trip him on his way. He still went. There are times I have chosen to walk alone, confident I knew better. I did not. There are many times I have wounded him deeply and times I have helped soothe the pain. I am ashamed of the many times in my life I have sinned, but I despise the times I remained lukewarm hoping to fly under the radar long enough to enjoy my happy life.

When I meditate, I truly try to visualize his suffering and make it as real as possible. I am so moved by the scene, I can close my eyes and imagine him close to me kneeling in fervent prayer. I try to place myself in the garden on that night, perhaps behind a rock or shrub, just taking it all in. I watch the man that I have come to love more than life itself, sweat blood because he has nothing else to give; he kneels, then falls to his face in hopes that it may be enough.

I listen to him plead with God, but submit without hesitation. I look at him and hear the concern, fear, and sincerity in every prayer he utters. He volunteers his tender heart for our jabs and Satan stands at the front of the line, landing low blow after low blow as he tries to pull Jesus under. I look around as if to urge someone to help him and see that he struggles all alone. He is so distressed that it tears at my heart and it is then that I finally understand how much he loves us. I do believe that if I could ever truly see that sight, I would fall to my face with a vow to never sin again, determined to never add more pain to his humble and earnest heart.

DISCUSSION CORNER

Meditate in silence for ten to fifteen minutes. Place yourself in the garden watching our Savior as he yearns for a way to reach us. He desires so much for us to understand his love that he submits to death on our behalf. There is no greater love.

Our sins—he can deal with those if we ask him, but the loss of our love, because of sin, torments him. Discuss the traps Satan uses to keep us from almighty and everlasting forgiveness.

HOW TO PRAY

We are so fortunate that, if so inclined, we may indulge ourselves in prayer at any time and in any place. It costs no money and is readily available to all who seek it. The channel to heaven is open, can be used on demand, single user to entire world with no bandwidth constraints. Each of us operates and manages his own free will and ruminations that may, at any time, invoke a prayer. We must learn how to shoot up prayers in places where it is sorely needed, such as . . . public school buildings or campuses, sporting events, rock concerts, bars, groceries, or shopping malls. Unless there is trouble, most of these locations do not prompt us to pray, yet the silent prayer is heard and rewarded. We should vow that wherever we are, so too is our prayer.

Read the passage below as it explains to us about prayer. We do not need to know "how to pray" as the Holy Spirit will transform our prayers into humble perfection, fit for the King.

> *In the same way, the Spirit too comes to the aid of our weakness; for we do not know how to pray as we ought, but the Spirit itself intercedes with inexpressible groanings. And the one who searches hearts knows what is the intention of the Spirit, because it intercedes for the holy ones according to God's will. Romans 8:26-27*

It is comforting to know a prayer is only a thought away, a mere shifting of reflections. Whatever it may be that triggers the spontaneous prayer, it serves an important purpose. It is a conscious effort to invoke God's presence in our lives. It may bring comfort to another, serve as a vessel for thanksgiving, or as an avenue for requests. If prayer may be seen as connecting us to heaven, a moment in prayer deducts time subjected to the trials of the world and adds time to refueling our souls with Truth through His holy peace.

Sometimes a firing off of little prayers throughout the day will suffice, but they fall short when the need is great. You cannot take an aspirin instead of having surgery, substitute a car wash for an oil change, or expect a fleeting prayer to help when you know you should be on your knees or flat on your face. Surrendering or humbling ourselves is pleasing to God because it allows Him to pick us up into His lap. Once there we can see the love in his eyes, hear the thump of his heart and feel the strength of His arms that surround us. We breathe when he breathes, move when He moves and become in synch with Him. Once we allow God to be in synch with us, we can endure anything.

There never has been, nor will be, any human closer to God than Jesus. Matthew and Mark help us visualize this critical prayer encounter between Son and Father . . . and it is beautiful. Please read Matthew 26: 39.

The position the Only Begotten Son of God chose to address his Father in Heaven was on his face, laying prostrate in perfect humility. Why do you think that Jesus chose to go face down in the Garden of Gethsemane? Are we that important to him and is our cause so grave? Yes and Yes. This was not the time for a pal-to-pal conversation, or even a son-to-father chat. This was Jesus demonstrating for us a form of perfect humility, submission and reverence; like the lamb laying down for slaughter. Jesus chose a physical position that he already knew would be pleasing to His Father and would match his level of request.

Now read Mark 14:36.

Jesus calls his Father by a name not used in the other gospels. It states, in the corresponding footnotes, "Abba" is Aramaic for a very intimate or special name between Jesus and his father, God. In English, perhaps it equates to calling our parent "dad" or "daddy," rather than using the more formal name of father. The other gospels may not have mentioned it because it translates to "father" anyway, but aren't you glad that it was preserved in Mark's gospel and not translated into oblivion?

Our lesson in all of this: Jesus pulls out all of the stops and teaches us how to pray and mean it. Jesus teaches us to ask for anything because, with all due respect, nothing is beyond God. Jesus allowed God to choose what he would and would not do with his life, keeping true to the faith that God can do the impossible. Jesus prays with an open and circumcised heart, he humbles himself by lying prostrate and chooses a most intimate name for his father. He shows us that when we humble ourselves, God can and will take us through anything.

Do you remember Luke 22:43, which we already read at the beginning of this chapter? It states that an angel of heaven was sent to strengthen him in the garden during his prayer. Believing that God would have been witnessing the intense humility of His Only Begotten Son's plea, and understanding His abundant outpouring of Fatherly love as the hour closed in on the one He loved, can you imagine the heavenly roar that roused the angel who would, without delay, come to Jesus' aid?

JUST ONE HOUR

I do not watch much television but there are a few shows I really like. The hour-long program just flies by leaving me wanting more and anxious for the next new episode. A movie in the theatre is even longer, lasting an hour and a half or two. A football or basketball game can last a few hours and sometimes leaves us on the edge of our seats as the final seconds tick away. Come to think of it, I have waited in doctors' offices or an emergency room lobby for far longer than an hour as I felt worried or bored out of my mind. I have even shown up an hour early to events so that I could secure a good seat. One-hour increments of time have been with us forever and neatly define segments of our lives. For the apostles, the night in the Garden of Gethsemane was for sure an hour to remember.

Please read Mark 14:37-41.

Do you ever wonder if the apostles thought about leaving out some of these passages that made them look heartless, ignorant, or futile? They were the authors and the storytellers so they had the ability to spin the truth how they saw fit. There were enough positives to share about their years with Jesus so no one would have missed a few incriminating tales. Why did they decide to include the times they were rebuked by Jesus (Luke 9:55), the time Peter had the audacity to rebuke Jesus and lived to regret it (Matthew 16: 22-23), the time they were too weak in their faith to remove a demon (Mark 9:18-19), and the time they fell asleep on the job? Especially after they found out the rest of the story, how bad does that make them look? Oh, how they probably stewed about this night, wondering why they denied Jesus such a small last request—to stay awake—JUST ONE HOUR!

After all they had been through together, they could not find the strength to pray beside him. Were they finding the evening boring? Only moments earlier they were sitting to witness the very first Eucharist being administered to man, and hearing **Jesus** declare the words that made it so. Wow! But they were missing something, for the Last Supper dishes had barely been cleared from the table when the apostles were placing themselves in "relax" mode.

Jesus' disciples were men who grew in integrity as they grew in faith. Jesus even warned them, "the spirit is willing but the flesh is weak." The disciples had a willing spirit, pointed toward God, but their earthly bodies and minds refused to follow. Man's willingness alone cannot overpower the mind and body; man with the Holy Spirit possess the strength to overcome the challenges of both mind and body as God fuels the soul within.

It was not until the disciples learned to fully empty themselves that the Spirit of God was able to fill them up, claiming residence in the body and soul of the warrior for God. The Holy Spirit must prevail over us for it is with our earthly mind and body we fail. Without God the disciples would have remained in a state of shame, hiding from their offenses. With God they saw their mistakes. The lessons they learned became the very reason to spotlight each of their disastrous flaws, hoping to brighten the trail for other lost souls heading the wrong way.

If the disciples of Jesus had excluded these passages two things could have happened. One, we would not be able to learn from their mistakes, see ourselves in their trials and learn the strategy to overcome human weakness. Secondly, and perhaps more damaging, we would have mistakenly ascertained that the first disciples were near perfect human beings and chosen by Jesus because of their righteousness. We would have missed the whole point Jesus was making about "qualifying the called" rather than "calling the qualified."

Take a look at the old pits that have caused you to stumble or fall and the progress you made when you reached up for God's hand to pull you out. With absolute certainty, know that with God nothing is impossible. And if you question this, re-read verses 39-41 to find the snoozing Apostles of Christ the <u>second</u> and the <u>third</u> time Jesus returned. Three times! And all of this happened in . . . about one hour.

There are one hundred sixty eight hours in a week. One hour represents less than 1% of our week. Sunday liturgy is about ONE hour in length. Ponder that for a moment. Attending Mass doesn't seem like such a lofty request, does it?

HUMAN SORROW

A broken leg gets a cast. A third degree burn gets salve and a bandage. Cancers and weakened hearts show up on X-rays and scans. Even the congestion of the common cold can be "heard" if not seen. A black eye or bruise remains for days after a blow but how can we see sorrow? What about the whack to the heart that hurts deeper than any of the above, may even last longer, yet provides no sign of its presence? It is easy to miss the signs of sorrow in someone's heart unless we search with God's eyes and listen with God's ears. It is difficult to articulate our own sorrow to someone else because the wound of sorrow is painful and complex, often rooting itself many years before the recent fertilization caused it to grow.

Even though God can, and does, use others to help us through our sorrows, many times, our deepest sorrow remains simply between God and us. It is in such a deep place that only He knows how to navigate to its core. Only He knows how to treat it and comfort it. Only He knows how to loosen the hold and set us free. Dealing with sorrow is where God excels . . . and no appointment is necessary to meet one-on-one with the Divine Physician. Come as you are and ask God to help you understand the sorrow and to gain the graces to deal with it. Jesus did. We can too.

Catholic Link

Catechism of the Catholic Church

1769 In the Christian life, the Holy Spirit himself accomplishes his work by mobilizing the whole being; with all its sorrows, fears and sadness, as is visible in the Lord's agony and passion. In Christ human feelings are able to reach their consummation in charity and divine beatitude.

The above Catholic Link packs a huge punch in a few very concise and well-chosen words. Read it over a few times to let it sink in.

GETHSEMANE 101

It may seem elementary, but those in need will understand. Most of us have experienced anxiety in some form. Maybe it lasted moments until it corrected itself or perhaps it plagues you on a weekly, nightly, or daily basis. **Jesus knows about anxiety.** Run to him for strength to endure the trials and ask for peace to overcome the darkness that closes in on you. Many times as I meditate on this sorrowful time for Jesus, I add a prayer for those who need some relief. I pray they may know peace, but also for them to know Jesus understands their deep and hidden pain.

He walked the path before us and can help with the burden if we call on him to do so. Perhaps this particular meditation will give them hope, for only our Creator knows from where each anxiety originated and how best to unravel the ball of troubles. Let us pray that he answers His children by leading them through the challenging maze to a place of peace.

Second Prayer: The Suffering on the Mount of Olives

The Prayer of St. Bridget for The Suffering on the Mount of Olives

Pray 1 Our Father, 1 Hail Mary, then:

Eternal Father, through Mary's unblemished hands and the Divine Heart of Jesus, I offer You the terrifying suffering of Jesus' Heart on the Mount of Olives and every drop of His Bloody Sweat as atonement for my and all of humanity's sins of the heart, as protection against such sins and for the spreading of Divine and brotherly Love.

The Flogging

Bible passages needed for study of this chapter:
Luke 23:15-16, 22   Isaiah 52:14   Psalm 22:17-19
Deuteronomy 25:1-3   Isaiah 53:5   Psalms 69:21
Isaiah 50:6   Wisdom 2:19   Matthew 27:11-25

Please read Luke 23:15-16, 22.

Pontius Pilate found no capital crime associated with the man, Jesus. What do these verses tell you about Pilate's original thought process for the way to handle the people's accusations? He first attempted to push him off under another's jurisdiction. When that failed, Pilate planned to appease the crowd with a Roman method of discipline known as flogging (or scourging) and then release him.

As I meditate on this time of blood shedding, I cannot help to wonder how easily this day could have shaped up differently. I can't help contemplating numerous unanswered questions. After all, what did happen to Pilate's scourge and release plan? When did he lose control of the crowd? Where did the groundswell come from that contributed to Jesus' demise? Wasn't Pilate warned that this might not be the way he wanted to be remembered? Why did this conviction not follow normal protocol? How did the glory of Palm Sunday turn into the shame of Good Friday? And possibly the most important question of all . . . what if God had changed his mind, turned from us in utter disappointment, and taken His Son to safety before this day would pass? We are blessed because of the outcome but there is much to study about the suffering of our Lord Jesus and the patience of the Father God who sent him.

We probably know the story of the Passion of Christ like the back of our hand but we are about to uncover even more about the dynamics of this day, to see how we fall into the same traps today and to realize that if even one calm head had prevailed . . . the day would have looked much different. That was not the will of God, however, and so it played out as it did and, by the way, exactly how the prophets foretold it. You would think the crowd would have known better. Instead, the day was shaping up to be a monumental disaster of unparalleled proportions as the enemy was allowed to run amuck, inciting the willing to slaughter the "Lamb" rather than release it.

When all hope looked lost as our Lord was condemned to death by the crowd and then authorized by Pontius Pilate, it was God who reserved the right to have the final say. And He would remain patient as the dreadful day painfully and slowly ticked away. What an excruciating day this would have been to witness. For his faithful followers, all goodness would have seemed shut out from the world as darkness enveloped the city that sentenced him to death.

THE TRAP, THEN AND NOW

God allowed Satan to unleash his fury of evil upon his first small but growing audience. That fury then instigated a torrent of unsettled jealousy, hatred and frustration that grew in intensity before landing on its victim, our Lord Jesus Christ. Here is a thought: What if the people consulted with God before making this rash decision? In other words, they had taken their issues of concern to the altar while they prayed for clarity and wisdom about the man called the Son of God. What if they had asked for direction instead of steering the ship into hell? Perhaps some did but were easily outnumbered, their voices drowned out by the ones taunted and driven by the evil one.

So many people fell into the trap laid by Satan that day. Have we not experienced the snare first-hand? Have you ever been "just mildly" disappointed in someone and then suddenly found yourself fuming hot? What provokes us to boil over—Was it a morning when the alarm clock failed or the last straw of an entire day gone wrong? Was it years of frustration penned up too long or a sudden injustice that consumed our every thought? Why do annoyances we normally can handle set us off? Like a gentle wave of ocean turned tsunami we buckle under its force within us.

It happens to me with those I love. It happens during confrontations when I give into the whispers that remind me of the ten other times they disappointed me or the day last week when I thought it best to "swallow" my words rather than unleash them. The almost-forgotten strife festers inside me like a helping of spoiled food, bubbling and gurgling until the unsettled mess expels from my mouth. I am shocked I actually said it! I initially defend it; later I regret it. And as it goes, it is ALWAYS much worse coming back up than it was going down.

One small flame, if not contained by the love of Christ, can blow up like a match on gasoline. We must be careful to include God in our discussions and confrontations, asking Him to guide us and to separate the drama from the reality we must deal with.

There is good news, however. Knowing how their hardened hearts would react, God used their wickedness to prove his love for us, to declare His perfect Son to us and to deliver us from every evil. He wiped our slate of debt clean, so to speak, with the blood of Jesus. Could God have not told us all of this without the sacrifice of His Only Begotten Son? He tried. We did not listen. His plea for us is to accept Him, hear His voice and follow Him. It sounds easy after you know what Jesus went through to prove it to us but there will be some who still decline the offer. There will be others who feel the trap they are in is too deep for a Savior to reach. Never underestimate the power of God.

All of this happened and was recorded in such excruciating detail for the purpose that we might choose to live eternity with the one who loved us, literally, to death.

> *For God so loved the world that he gave his only Son, so that everyone who believes in him might not perish but might have eternal life. John 3:16*

> *See what love the Father has bestowed on us that we may be called the children of God. Yet so we are. The reason the world does not know us is that it did not know him. 1 John: 3:1*

DISCUSSION CORNER

Discuss among the group times you lost your temper and times you were pleased with the way you handled conflict. Consider the triggers that snap you and the peace that affords you clarity. Why do you think people react differently to similar situations? In other words, how can one not even notice, another simmer and yet a third boil over at the same set of circumstances? What words or actions prompt you to deviate from your normal path of rational thinking? Discuss the similarities and differences among the group and share techniques each uses to address conflicts and diffuse unconstructive rage. Finally, pray together that we will come to know the enemy's playbook for attacking our individual vulnerabilities and ask for God's coaching as we prepare, strengthen, and execute our own defense.

THE PUNISHMENT

The punishment of flogging or scourging was biblical and written about in the book of Deuteronomy. Please read Deuteronomy 25:1-3. According to the Jewish law, if convicted of a crime, one could receive "stripes" in accordance with the severity of the crime committed. The maximum number of stripes was 40 and it even states the reason for the limitation.

I grew up thinking that Jesus was whipped 40 times, in accordance with this law, until I learned about Roman torture. The Romans set no boundaries such as the Jewish law. It is written into history the Romans were especially brutal in their delivery of punishment and perfected techniques to bring countless criminals to near death before stopping. (note 3-1) They used scourging as both a punishment for a crime and a precursor to crucifixion. The scourging instruments themselves were made for maximum cruelty, weaving bone and metal into the leather straps to more readily rip at the flesh of their subject. The wounds would be inflicted across the back and extending upwards to the shoulders. They stood near him as they unleashed the whip that landed on the exposed and vulnerable back of the man. They would continue, unrelenting and with increased power, as was the job of the Roman lictor. It was not until the overseer (centurion) would signal, that the beating would halt. Jesus was not persecuted under Jewish law; he was indeed persecuted by the worst of the worst, the Ancient Roman Empire.

We do not know exactly how long the beating persisted but other scripture passages give us indications as to how heavy were the sins of mankind that fell repeatedly upon the back of our Most Holy Savior. The atonement process began as the Lamb of God stood silently for the beating. For the lictors, this silence and lack of pleading for one's life would have enraged them even more for the measuring stick of their own delight through audible triumph would not have been met. For this they would have compensated the audible loss with visual gratification, beating upon him with more vengeance to justify their manliness in front of their peers and authorities.

Read each of the Old Testament prophesies listed below and then read my notes for an abbreviated description. My notes will remind you as you flip the pages but they do not have the same impact reading will. I pray this exercise will help as we piece together important events in the Passion of Christ. Because New Testament writers knew their readers were familiar with the practice of Roman crucifixion they spared us some of the gruesome details, however the prophets help us pull it back into view.

Isaiah 50:6, He submitted to beatings and spitting

Isaiah 52:14, He was marred beyond recognition

Isaiah 53:5, He was pierced, crushed and scourged to heal us

Wisdom 2:19, He was tortured and they tested his patience to prove his gentleness

Psalms 22:17-19 (17), His hands and feet were wasted.

(18), His bones exposed to counting. They gloated and stared at him.

(19), They gambled for his clothes.

Psalms 69:21, Broken-hearted and weak, he was lonely from the lack of compassion.

So how is it the Old Testament can hold keys to a crucifixion that happened in New Testament times? Remembering that all of these passages were written hundreds of years before Jesus was born, it is difficult for us to understand how such writings could come to be. It begs the question: why did they not recognize the Messiah when he was standing right in front of them? Perhaps it is for many reasons, two of which I will offer you now.

One reason is because they simply did not want to see. Many of those who awaited the Messiah would have already "dreamed up" an image of their king. It is understandable that they would use earthly measures of power to create a vision of an invincible man. This "image" of the Messiah gave hope to the Jewish faithful as they fell deeper and deeper into persecution. No doubt he would be fierce, dynamic, feared, and rebellious. He would bring nations to their knees and silence all opposition. He would be a commander and a military genius. With the Messiah leading them, there would be no more persecution and the Jewish people would live without fear and without rejection.

They did not want to believe that a poor carpenter with no authority could fill that dream. Hundreds of years of persecution had seared an image of hope into their minds, and that image looked more like a king than a carpenter, born into royalty rather than humility, waging war rather than sewing peace. He was nothing like the God they had feared and followed. He was loving and compassionate to all. He wore plain clothes and mingled with sinners. He did not seek their riches, their authority, or their approval to gain popularity. He WAS a different kind of king.

Another reason may be because God's prophets wrote in riddles, concealing the truth until the "Truth" played out. God did not provide a checklist of Messiah characteristics, but instead wove foretelling images of Christ into many books announcing the Messiah, leaving faith as the only key to solve the riddle. Those with preconceived Messiah images would fall victim to their own fantasies whereas the faithful would wait for God to fill their eyes with the image they yearned for. Scripture verses throughout the Old Testament reveal to us the death of Jesus and the suffering that he accepted on our behalf, however, they were not a road map to identifying our Savior. Even the apostles, who lived in the moment of Christ, had a difficult time piecing together the hidden messages until the New Covenant was fully established by Jesus. Then, the loose threads of Old Testament prophecies began weaving into the rest of the story. If not for the valiant efforts of the New Testament authors and our God who breathed the words to life, we would lack much clarity and understanding.

TAKING A BEATING FOR THOSE WHO BEAT YOU

This is one of the toughest lessons for me to grasp: Jesus allowed himself to be beaten so that even his tormentors might know salvation. Jesus took one for the team, so to speak, so that members of the other team could also win? This one hurts my head as I think about how far away I am from understanding and practicing this deep form of humility, sacrifice, and forgiveness. When Jesus came to earth, he came for all of mankind. He prayed for the hands that beat him, the mouths that mocked him, the legs that kicked him, and the strength that pulled at him as he was nailed to the cross. Jesus does not pray for evil in the world, as Scripture points out in John 17:9, but he prays for the men, women, and children of this world that belong to God but are provoked by evil. He yearned for his tormentors in spite of the physical assault unleashed upon his human body. Do you think, however, the pain our current generation inflicts upon his "heavenly body" is any less hurtful?

What is your threshold for pain and when do you stop praying for your tormentors and for those who torment your loved ones? Some may honestly say that they never stop praying for them because they never began in the first place! Others may claim they stop when, in their opinion, the person is too far-gone. Others may humbly murmur that they never stop because they are moved to pray for all those who are in most need of His gracious mercy.

Jesus teaches us that prayer is not an exclusive hobby but rather an inclusive way of life in him. He demonstrates here how difficult it is to love our enemy, but in doing so we are more like him. The commandment that Jesus gave to us is all-inclusive as it states that we should love one another . . . as he has loved us. (Cf. John 14:34) We do not get to select those we wish to consider as part of the "one another", because Jesus did not choose one over the other. He loved us all, died for us all and was resurrected for us all so that whoever chooses him shall have eternal life.

As our Creator, God made us to desire Him so that He alone can fill the heart that hungers for something more. We know that God rejoices when even one soul repents, turns from evil and begins a new life with Him. Then if God does rejoice He too must feel the opposite when we flee from Him. Like the prodigal son left his father (Luke 15:11-32) we too can exercise that option, but God does not will that life for us. Away from him we are vulnerable and empty. Even one lost sheep will raise His concern for He loves each one of us individually and graciously. We are not a percentage to Him—as if He would be content winning the majority! Not even 99.9 percent pacifies His will. **EVERY** soul is known and loved by God. He yearns for our return but will also accept our right to refuse Him.

IN TOO DEEP

Have you ever found yourself backpedaling, painted into a corner or so frustrated with the turn of events that it was easier to give-in than fight your way out? Every time you opened your mouth matters just worsened. Literally, there was no way out—or so you believed at the time—so you buckled. After, however, with a clear mind and alleviated tension you were able to think of a dozen better choices than the one you felt forced to make. Sometimes you later think of the perfect words you wished had come to your mind sooner. So, why do we cave-in?

Extreme pressure can cause *reactions* to circumstances rather than follow a course of normal *actions*. Caught in the moment, we block out all options as we struggle to simply survive. Human nature is to survive and so the body must be trained to stay cool under pressure, remain strong to our principles and weigh the options. Pontius Pilate did not get his job as a Roman Governor by being soft. So what caused him to give-in to the pressure and change direction?

Matthew 27:11-25 helps us understand the events preceding the verdict. Each gospel contains a bit about the thoughts and actions of Pontius Pilate, but let's study Matthew for an overall snapshot of the day gone wrong. Please read it and then let's look for important clues to his frame of mind.

In verse 13 it appears that Pilate was attempting to remind Jesus this was not a simple misdemeanor crime he was charged with. Pilate was looking for a way out of the monumental mess and turned to Jesus for a little help or possibly some clarification. He hoped for a morsel, instead he got silence. The defense Pilate hoped to build was slipping fast. With nothing to go on, there could be no spin tactic in hopes of an acquittal and nothing Pilate could "clear up" in hopes to pacify the angry crowd. Yet Pilate still did not give up.

Like a magician trick loosing steam, then remembering he had a card up his sleeve, Pilate got one more crack at justice! Attempting to reconcile his doubts of guilt and save face, he chose the infamous Barabbas to pit against Jesus for the annual prison release holiday. He convinced himself the crowd had made their point, accomplished their goal to hush the man and would now be satisfied with a weaker punishment for Jesus.

Yes, Pontius Pilate planned to seal the deal by offering a criminal they detested against the release of Jesus. Surely they would see their misjudgment when comparing the man who gave and saved to the one who robbed and destroyed. Pilate, now proud of his ingenuity, thought: *Cooler heads will certainly prevail and I may even make it home early tonight for the holiday! I could surprise my lovely wife with a bottle of fine wine and . . .* But before he could complete the thought a note was delivered to him. He must have been on her mind too because the note was clearly in her writing. The warning was unambiguous and explicable. She warned the one she loved to walk away from the trap.

This, above all, would have caused Pilate to reconsider his position. It is ironic that while she suffered through a dream, revealing the innocence of Jesus, her husband suffered through the reality of crucifying him. It makes sense why Pilate, warned by his beloved, continued to guard the innocence of Jesus until the end.

Pilate lost the Barabbas battle rather quickly but still had to do something with Jesus. With still a sliver of hope that the crowd would be lenient he offered them the chance to redeem themselves. Instead, the trap became wider as it lowered on top of the man who lost his chance to run away. The shouts were in unison, commanding and clear. They had chosen crucifixion for the innocent man and this is when I believe Pilate lost his chance to reconcile the crowd.

In verse 23 Pilate asked them for a reason, but the crowd gave no response other than the demand for crucifixion. A governor does not condemn a man because a few people say he is guilty. If that were the case, Barabbas would have been dead a long time ago and there would be no prisoners to release on the holiday. Was it the size of the crowd that frightened Pilate or the stature of the people within the crowd? Pilate lost the battle when he did not slam the door on their unfounded accusations, seem appalled at their outrageous request and remain firm in due process. The riot ensued before him as they took advantage of his vulnerable and feeble state.

Then he remembers the warning of the wife he loves coupled with a gut feeling this man is not an imposter. He attempts to disown the very words he alone has forced upon himself and in verse 24 he visually demonstrates his guiltlessness by washing his hands before the crowd. That gesture may have made him feel better but the permanent stain on his reputation was recorded forever. The man, who held the power of life or death, spoke life but condoned death. The outcome is still death. Death is permanent.

Unfortunately, for most decisions we make there is no turning back. Time has soaked up the error like the sun evaporates a puddle. Our secret seemingly safe within the clouds for a short time will drench us with a thunderstorm a few days later. There is no way to undo what was done, fix the damage, unsay what was said or change the outcome of the chain of events we set in motion. In other words, no matter how much Pontius Pilate may have regretted his actions, one cannot "un-crucify" the crucified.

The gospel of John gives us one more piece of information that may have contributed to Pilate's decision. Please read John 19:10-12, 15:

> So Pilate said to him, "Do you not speak to me? Do you not know that I have power to release you and I have power to crucify you?" Jesus answered [him], "You would have no power over me if it had not been given to you from above. For this reason the one who handed me over to you has the greater sin." Consequently,

> *Pilate tried to release him; but the Jews cried out, "If you release him, you are not a Friend of Caesar. Everyone who makes himself a king opposes Caesar."... They cried out, "Take him away, take him away! Crucify him!" Pilate said to them, "Shall I crucify your king?" The chief priests answered, "We have no king but Caesar."*

When the chief priests pulled out the Caesar card, I believe this raised the stakes. Pontius Pilate did not want to deal with a riot nor have to answer questions regarding one in his territory. But above all, he could not be linked to releasing a direct threat to Caesar. That would be political suicide and a personal death wish. The Sanhedrin, having lost ability to put anyone to death, needed the governor's authority and therefore leaned heavily and relentlessly upon him.

DISCUSSION CORNER

Each of us has experienced power at some level—whether a CEO of a large company, a coach or captain of a sports team, a manager at a quaint café or a babysitter on a Saturday night—we have held authority over others that count on us to do right by them.

Discuss the strengths and vulnerabilities inherent in human power. In your opinion, what relationship does power share with responsibility? Pilate's moment of weakness allowed the chief priests and elders to use his authority to speed up conviction and ensure a Roman penalty of crucifixion. Many people who hold powerful positions are targets for derailment. Why do they need our prayers?

Close by praying for the protection and right judgment of your leaders and for yourself when you are asked to lead. I pray that God may place those leaders most in need of protection on your heart this day.

HOW FAR WOULD YOU ASK SOMEONE TO GO FOR YOU?

Delegating is one thing but asking someone to take a hit for you is another. When I first thought about this notion, I was quick to react that I would never ask anyone to take a hit for me. I live in a rather safe area and I am not in a position of importance to require bodyguards. If I simply mind my own business and do not place myself in dangerous situations, I will probably be just fine. *Thanks, but no thanks. I've got this one.*

Then I thought of the reason I feel safe in my town and remembered the police, fire and emergency crews that safeguard us 24/7. Then I remembered the people who keep the lights on, the water running and the gas pumps filled. I would not feel as safe if I was in the dark, thirsty and had no fuel for warmth, cooking or travel. I think of the doctors studying long hours so they can "fix" us, and the lab technicians that read our test results with concentration and resolve. I think of the military men and women who keep us safe at home and overseas. I remember my own mom and dad who sacrificed all their life so they could give each of us kids a solid start. How simplistic I was making my independence in a world that truly is anything but.

We may never know all of the "things" we do not have to "bother" with because of the beating our Lord Jesus took that day. To look upon his scourging and to imagine his obedient silence at the pillar is to know how much he loves us. Gaze into the weary eyes that yearn for your glance. Look upon the parched lips that have whispered your name. Concentrate on the bound hands that now can reach to you from your darkness. Watch him accept the blow only a man in love could endure. Find his tormentors tools and you see the sins that offend him. Find the blood dripping from his back and you see the richness that cleansed us from our sins. Before it was done, every ounce of his blood would be shed so that we could live. The slaughter of the lamb—the blood of the lamb—sacrificed for us so that we would not have to be bothered.

Open the Catholic Link as if it were a heavenly present personally delivered by an angel to you. Your name is hand-written with glistening stars on the tag tied to the heart of the bow. Oh how He wants us to know how much He loves us . . .

Catholic Link

Catechism of the Catholic Church

614 This sacrifice of Christ is unique; it completes and surpasses all other sacrifices.[441] First, it is a gift from God the Father himself, for the Father handed his Son over to sinners in order to reconcile us with himself. At the same time it is the offering of the Son of God made man, who in freedom and love offered his life to his Father through the Holy Spirit in reparation for our disobedience.[442]

[441] Cf. *Heb* 10:10. [442] Cf. *Jn* 10:17-18; 15:13; *Heb* 9:14; *1 Jn* 4:10.

A DIFFERENT KIND OF LONELY

A True Story . . .

It was Mother Teresa who first introduced me to the notion that a person can be in the middle of a crowded city, in a room full of family, in a high school as big as a college campus or a celebrity with a million fans . . . and still be lonely. It didn't make sense to me. I spent a great deal of my life hoping to experience loneliness. Growing up with a family of seven in a roughly 1600 sq. ft. home, I yearned for a little alone time. Every corner I turned produced another family member. I could search but would mostly never find a quiet place to retreat. In fact, even when we took a shower we had to leave the door unlocked so there was always access to the toilet if needed. Four of us kids were born in the span of six years so we grew up shoulder-to-shoulder and arm-in-arm. We loved each other and tolerated each other. Sometimes we fought but I was never lonely.

When I first got my apartment I was so excited. I had the whole place to myself. It was difficult financially to make it without a roommate but I was determined to capture what had eluded me since birth . . . some time by myself.

I had moved about an hour away from my small hometown to the big city. I loved my freedom at first—basking in the glory of eating cake for breakfast, drinking beer for dinner and leaving clothes in the middle of the floor. It was liberating to know I could come and go as I pleased and no one would question me. (This was all before cell phone technology so when I was not at work or at home I was truly unreachable.) Then it occurred to me one day that if no one knew where I was, then how will they know to worry about me if I don't come home? A twinge of feeling completely alone finally entered my world but I still was not lonely. My parents and siblings were a phone call away and they always answered my calls—usually on the first ring! (Maybe they were a bit concerned.) I also made new friends, some of whom were life-long keepers, so I ditched being alone and added a string of fun roommates. A few years after that I traded them in for a husband and have not been alone since.

When I reflect on my past I realize the alone time I initially sought had nothing to do with loneliness. It never does. Lonely is different than being alone. I never felt lonely because I always knew I was loved.

"Loneliness and the feeling of being unwanted is the most terrible poverty." Mother Teresa

Yes, Mother Teresa actually categorized loneliness as poverty, and not just any poverty but the most terrible of poverties. Wealthy countries are not immune to this poverty and often times breed the worst cases. Mother Teresa talked about loneliness stemming from feeling unwanted, neglected, unloved and unneeded. What a dreadful place to be. How can people feel self-worth when they truly believe no one cares whether they live or die? The sad thing is, many times they are correct in their assumption. It is not so much that we do not care about them as it is our ignorance and blindness to loneliness. We ignore or mask the symptoms, believing the lonely are tended to with food and a bed. Money may hush the moans and stop the crying, but dignity is what they are starved for.

I realize why so many times Mother Teresa spoke to us about extending our hand to someone, touching them or picking them up into our arms. Her mission was always to restore dignity to those stripped of it. If dignity is held captive in loneliness then can it not be freed through personal interaction? That is where she found Jesus and that is where she urges us to turn our attention. How different the world would look if everyone felt loved, needed and wanted. In other words, if not one person suffered from the poverty of loneliness. Is this really such a lofty goal for a world as astute and progressive as we are? Why do we fail to recognize the desperate even when they live in our own town, neighborhood or house?

Volunteers often speak of feeling blessed by the people they have brought aid to, so they continue to volunteer because it feels good to do so. Unfortunately, not all needy in the world are kind and grateful. For Mother Teresa and the Congregation of the Missionaries of Charity, they know of this first-hand. We should remember their struggles because it will help us see beyond the thick walls created by loneliness. The missionaries seek to serve even those who continually refuse them, praying to God for help to recognize Jesus behind their "unattractive disguises". This is one such prayer the missionaries say:

> *Dearest Lord, may I see you today and every day in the person of your sick, and, whilst nursing them, minister unto you. Though you hide yourself behind the unattractive disguise of the irritable, the exacting, the unreasonable, may I still recognize you, and say: "Jesus, my patient, how sweet it is to serve you." Mother Teresa*

". . . how **sweet** it is to serve you?" Oh, may those be the words to ring in our ears forever. To serve the mean-hearted would not be an easy task; they take without giving back. There would be no satisfaction or sweetness in serving them, as it is when we are serving the grateful. Mother Teresa served them because Jesus served them. In the eyes of Jesus even the ungrateful are worthy.

As I meditate on the scourging I feel how lonely these hours were for Jesus, yet he allowed it to be done to him so we might trust and follow him. He knows loneliness and he knows the cure. When we follow him we become

56

his hands, his eyes and his ears. We can become part of the cure as we seek for the hidden Jesus in each person we encounter. If only we would turn our heads toward him who calls us to action. At the pillar stood a man who went to extremes to get our attention.

I AM SORRY, DEAR JESUS

Please pray: Dear Jesus, how loved we feel right now! Meditating on this physical scourging helps us see your face. We think of the times you lower your head because of the pain across your back and we see you raise your eyes again between blows. What are you looking for, dear Jesus? You look so very lonely standing tethered to the pillar that keeps you in place, and so far away from those who love you. We know that you stand there for all of us. Let not our days on Earth add to your suffering, but may your message live strong in our hearts. Teach us, oh Lord, to accept the cross that bears our name. Give us the strength to stand as you stood, through all pain and suffering. For if we choose to duck the blow, who behind us will not be protected from its force?

Third Prayer: The Flogging

The prayer of St. Bridget for the Flogging

Pray 1 Our Father, 1 Hail Mary, then:

Eternal Father, through Mary's unblemished hands and the Divine Heart of Jesus, I offer You the many thousands of Wounds, the gruesome Pains, and the Precious Blood of the Flogging as atonement for my and all of humanity's sins of the Flesh, as protection against such sins and the preservation of innocence, especially among my relatives.

The Crowning of Thorns

Bible passages needed for study of this chapter:

Mt. 27:27-31	Isaiah 48:17	Mark 2:1-12
Luke 19:41-42	Acts 7:54-60	John 20:23
Luke 18:32-34	Daniel 2:21-22	2 Corinthians 5:18

Please read Matthew 27:27-31

Pontius Pilate hands Jesus over to be crucified and the soldiers lead him away to prepare him for his execution. What happens next is truly quite out of the ordinary.

According to a Bible commentary (note 4-1), the Romans normally followed a due process following conviction. A law enacted by the Roman senate required that criminals sentenced to execution be given at least 10 days to prepare for their deaths and to handle their affairs. Again, our Lord received no such consideration. Instead of time to gather his thoughts, prepare for his death or nearly even exhale a breath, he was whisked away to a room within the praetorium. The praetorium is the residence of a governor or high-ranking leader.

Such a government locale should have been regimented in lawful practice and should have provided Jesus a shelter from the mob outside and perhaps even a moment to recollect himself. However, as the irony of the day continues, Jesus' conviction forgoes laws of due process and deferred executions in exchange for a brutal display of mental belittling, harassment and public humiliation.

In verse 27 the gospel of Matthew states the "whole cohort" was invited to watch the humiliation of Jesus. The footnotes in the NAB Bible state that a cohort would normally be comprised of six hundred men. We cannot be sure what portion of the cohort was present on that day, but we do know the numbers would have been somewhat inflated from a normal day because of the increased security needed to cover the Jewish holiday. Therefore, you can imagine the crowd's energy as they jeered at Jesus and spurred onward the soldiers who tormented him.

Reading verses 28 and 31, when paying close attention to the chronological order of Jesus' crucifixion day, may cause you to flinch. If, as scripture leads us to believe, the order of events was such that Jesus first was scourged then mocked—an appalling implication lies within these verses. After enduring the brutal scourging, Jesus' clothes were placed back on him. The soldiers, so they could mock him, stripped him. Think of a piece of cotton laid over an open wound for a short time and then ripped off. His tunic would have been pressed against the severely beaten back of our Lord. This would have caused him pain yet probably served as a dam, temporarily stopping the outward flow of blood from his wounds. Any progress his body made to thwart the loss of blood would have ended with the painful re-exposure as his clothes were once again stripped from his body. Add a heavy military cloak to the open wounds and it creates a very painful experience. Then, in verse 31, from his raw back the military cloak was removed and his own clothes were put on *again*!

It continues to get worse. Verse 29 speaks of the crown of thorns woven by the soldiers and then placed upon the head of Jesus. The sharpness of the thorns would cause puncture wounds around his delicate head, causing more blood to be spent as ransom for our sinfulness. The pain would be excruciating yet he would allow it.

As you meditate on this sorrow allow yourself to imagine the sounds in the room when the crown of thorns was first presented to the crowd. Is it first hoisted in the air so the crowd can roar before it is placed upon his sacred head? Can you hear the soldiers' spiteful catcalls as they build in momentum? Imagine the destructive energy in the room as each soldier desperately tries to outdo the one before, using vulgarity and humiliation to rip apart Our Savior.

We have been in situations like this before, when meanness takes on a life of its own and cruelty becomes the sport for competition. We do not know the name of the soldier credited with the idea to gather a vine of thorns to weave into a crown, but we know the evil voice that prompted him. It is the same disgusting voice that leads us to begin or join discussions of gossip, plot ways for revenge against someone who has hurt us and tear apart those we have judged unworthy.

(That last sentence reminds me of a story, actually something I experienced. Let's finish this scripture passage first, then I'll share it with you.)

In verse 29 we are also introduced to the reed they made Jesus hold and the sacrilegious way they knelt before, and mocked, the true Prince of Peace. Doesn't your heart ache when you think of this display of cruelty?

If it weren't enough to physically abuse him, they would take this opportunity to further destroy his spirit through attacking him mentally. Because it is so personal, mocking someone is especially effective when trying to break the person down. Where physical abuse ends mental abuse begins as it attacks the body in its entirety. The more personal the accusation is, the deeper the blow to one's humanity. The soldiers of the cohort took all that was good and ripped it apart. As if they had laid open his tender heart, they were plucking out every good gesture, miracle and spoken word; then using it against him. The soldiers were making a joke of his holy life.

Still the soldiers must not have been satisfied because in verse 30 they began spitting upon him. This is one of the lowest forms of humiliation and shame. It is a disgusting and spiteful practice demonstrating the highest form of disrespect. What had Jesus done to them to cause such an outrage? He had done nothing. He was an innocent man taking upon him the sins of mankind so we may know how much we are loved.

He chose to walk this path of hardship so we might trust him to lead us through our own hardships. No matter how bad it gets, Jesus has felt it and feels it along with us. He understands our pain, suffering and sorrow. He knows because he was there, enduring it all with silence and resolution, hoping that we would have enough faith to follow him who conquered death for our salvation.

A DAY AT THE POOL

A True Story . . .

I promised a story, so here it is. I have not told anyone of this experience before now yet it has greatly influenced me throughout the years. I never even thought about sharing it—until I wrote the paragraph about the cohort of soldiers abusing Jesus and the one attention-seeking soldier who thought to weave the crown of thorns. This story has become a part of my regrets in life but also an experience of humility.

I was a teenager from a small mid-western town just trying to fit in with a new crowd of friends. I remember feeling as if I had "outgrown" my old friends; they were boring to me. I watched and yearned for a life with a bit more exposure to the "popular" folk. A few girls from the new and improved crowd asked me to go to the public pool with them and I was elated. It wasn't long into our day of swimming that I became paranoid. I was sure they were going to think me a nerd because I was struggling to keep up with their colorful conversations. I felt as if I had just crawled out from under a rock, so naïve to their small town worldliness. It was late in the day that the chance to redeem myself came.

A group of girls that we liked to call "hoods" were conversing in the shallow end of the pool within earshot of us. They were part of a rougher crowd consisting of the smokers and the fighters at our school. One of the girls I was with began to make fun of them. Oh, how that got some attention. Another joined in. The laughter escalated. I was impressed with how easily amused my new friends were. After all, I grew up with two older brothers that used to relentlessly tease me so this was one area I had some expertise. I can't remember exactly what I said but it had something to do with the tallest girl's flat chest. My companions all looked at me in amazement—*did those words just come out of the mouth of the new girl?* It must have had merit because they all repeated the slam, each emphasizing different words to gain yet a bigger laugh. I knew I was finally "in" yet I felt miserable inside.

My new friends left the pool a few minutes before my mom was supposed to pick me up. I remember walking into the dressing room by myself and it was very quiet. I reached into my locker and found my clothes, stuffed them in my bag and turned around. I had not heard them come in but they were all there. The hoods had followed me into the dressing room and they were staring me down. Hoping it was just a coincidence that they were leaving at the exact same time I was, I began to walk around them so they could get to their lockers. They blocked me from leaving.

The tallest girl started in on me. She was daring me to repeat the words that came so freely to my lips just minutes before. She accused me of being scared as I stood alone, and I was. She yelled at me for making fun of her and she threatened me with physical abuse. They had me cornered. This was not going to end well.

I do not know from where the voice came but one of the girls with her spoke up. Her words were directed at me, saying something like . . . "I didn't think you were that kind of person." That single comment seemed to momentarily suck the venom from the room and I seized the opportunity to walk away. I had cleared several steps toward the doorway leading out. I was only moments from seeing my mom sitting in the tan station wagon (with faux wood on the sides) waiting to pick up her girl from the pool. She would most likely be smiling and asking me all about my day. I couldn't wait to see her.

Suddenly my head jerked back so hard that I staggered to regain my footing. Into her hand, the tall girl had clutched my long frizzy strands and pulled so tightly I thought more of my hair would end up in her hand then on my head. I turned myself back around toward the doorway and did not look back again but I clearly heard her last warning.

I don't remember saying anything on the way home. I probably just commented that I had a good time and left it at that. My mom probably didn't register my silence as a bad thing but rather chalked it up to me being a teenager.

I received two gifts that day. One was from the girl who recognized me from school where I tended to be kind to others and a bit on the shy side. She changed the mood in the room which allowed me to pass. The other came in the form of a jolt. The tall girl humbled me. I had hurt her with my words and she let me know it. I respect her for that and if she is out there, perhaps reading this, I want to tell her I am sorry for what I said and I will never forget her . . . and, of course, thank her for not beating me to a pulp.

DISCUSSION CORNER

We could perform an examination of our conscience at this point and further dwell on our huge mistakes in life but let's not. Let's discuss the peacemakers and the heroes; you know, the ones with true courage.

Peacemakers and heroes spend their selfless lives watching and learning from others. They are often quiet observers who fill their hearts with compassion for other human beings; never realizing compassion is what fuels true courage. Compassion gives us the reason to care what happens and wisdom is the check and balance for our emotions. God tempers compassion with wisdom but uses both to call us to action when a peacemaker or a hero is required to . . . run into a building of flames, save a child in harm's way, defend the country's freedom, turn the tide of gossip away, be a beggar for the poor, tell an intoxicated friend he can't drive, offer a different solution, save the party girl from the wolves closing in on her, calm the tension, sit at the lunch table with the person no one will sit with, be intolerant of any injustice and stop the needless fight (especially in the bathroom at the pool).

Courage is a spontaneous reaction to defend what we value. If we value virtue and righteousness then we will defend it. If we value human life then we will defend it. If we need more courage then possibly we simply need to love more deeply, with more compassion and with the same determination as our Savior, Jesus Christ.

Talk about courage in your group. Talk about the peacemakers and heroes of our time. In what areas are you already courageous and where do you wish you were more courageous? Do you tend to bury your compassion when you are faced with fear? Have you encountered a personal hero or peacemaker? Have you been one yet today? (Be attentive to your call to courage because, in this world, opportunities await each one of us daily!)

Below are a few quotes to stimulate conversation:

> *"Courage is not simply one of the virtues, but the form of every virtue at the testing point." C. S. Lewis*

> *"Courage is grace under pressure." Ernest Hemingway*

> *"Courage is found in unlikely places." J. R. R. Tolkien*

> *'Courage is fear holding on a minute longer." George S. Patton*

THE MIND'S GATEKEEPER

We were all created in God's image and we share with God both the ability and capacity to reason. God communicates to us through our reasoning yet God's reason is universal in nature, pure in thought and perfectly planned. Human reason is narrow in focus and limited in imagination. Its logic can be easily blocked or manipulated by our own selfish desires. Therefore, human reasoning cannot stand alone when it is the will of God we seek.

We require the gifts of the "divine gatekeeper," or Holy Spirit, to interpret and filter our reasoning. Lucky for us, these gifts are available to us through the Sacrament of Confirmation. Faith is the only requirement for opening, recognizing and retaining these gifts. The seven gifts of the Holy Spirit are: Wonder and Awe in God's Presence, Wisdom, Understanding, Right Judgment, Courage, Knowledge and Reverence.

Scripture passages speak many stories relating to the human being's intellectual side while placing God as the gatekeeper. Let's review a few to understand His ways and how he works within us to lead, protect and teach us. Read each scripture, look for God's almighty hand in it and then read the notes for each passage.

> **God protects us until we have the courage to make it—**
> Please read Luke 18:32-34 entitled The Third Prediction of the Passion. God chose to delay the apostles' understanding when they heard the paralyzing words of Christ's own death, yet allowed them to recall it later when the New Covenant had been fully revealed. God did not will the apostles to flee in terror at the news because he wanted them to witness the resurrection. This prediction, along with the mentoring words from the risen Christ, allowed the hearts and minds of the apostles to further blossom in faith and commitment.
>
> **God allows hardened hearts to remain concealed from His Son**—Please read Luke 19:41-42. Jesus laments for Jerusalem as he enters the city along with his disciples. Although Jesus is hailed as their king and revered by the growing crowds of people, he knows this city is like a wayward child. He weeps

for the many who will allow true peace to elude them for their faith is shallow and weak. Although God does not provoke us to blindness toward peace, He can and will allow it to evade us when we will not change our persistent disbelief, unfaithful spirit and stubborn behavior. Jesus knows the seeds planted in the people's hearts during this grand ceremonial entrance, triumph and proclamation will not last long on their hardened soil of doubt.

God wants to be close to us—Please read Isaiah 48:17. Isaiah tells us God not only will walk through life with us, but that he will lead the way. If we follow Him, He will also be our teacher. And what do teachers do? They prompt us to learn knowledge and wisdom through stimulating our minds and hearts. They blaze pathways to develop our judgment and aid in our maturity as human beings. There is no wiser teacher than the One who created us, knowing how best we absorb information and using every conceivable and inconceivable avenue to reach us.

God rewards His followers and uses everything for His glory—Please read Acts 7:54-60. This account of Stephen's martyrdom is an excellent depiction of how the Holy Spirit works within us, strengthening us through the challenges we may face in following the will of God. Stephen's courage and reverence came from his abundant faith, and God did not disappoint him at his death. Stephen was able to proclaim with awe, the amazing vision revealed to him only moments before his martyrdom. Although a brutal death of stoning awaited him, he chose to die like Jesus did—forgiving his tormentors. This scripture passage also introduces us to the young man named Saul (verse 58). Saul guarded the coats of Stephen's persecutors while they threw the stones to kill him. Saul witnessed the persecution of the first martyr for Jesus, yet his mind would be delayed from processing what his eyes had just witnessed (Acts 22:20). Saul, after hunting down and persecuting many Christians, finally converted his heart and his name "on the road to Damascus" (Acts 9). This conversion really paid off for the man we now regard as "St. Paul."

God answers prayers in big ways—Please read Daniel 2:21-22. This was Daniel's last chance to convince King Nebuchadnezzar that he was a useful and worthy citizen of Babylon. It was really quite simple, for if Daniel failed this test he, along with many others in the kingdom, would be put to death. The king was haunted by a terrible recurring dream and needed the dream to be interpreted for him so that he could have some peace. You may think this sounds easy; after all, Daniel could have created a plausible story that fit the dream and hoped the king believed him. But the unfair king demanded the interpreter not only reveal the meaning of the dream, but also the dream itself. Many pleaded with the king that this was impossible for anyone, but Daniel's faith instructed him to call upon God to answer the mystery. God chose to reveal both the dream and the meaning to Daniel so the king might spare his life. What you read in the scripture passage was Daniel's gratitude toward and reverence for God, whose great light revealed what was hidden in the darkness. You might say Daniel was "in awe."

This meditation, on the blood shedding of Christ Jesus through the crown of thorns, helps us understand the true nature of the mental attack he endured. These outrageous accusations were blows to the being, or soul, of Christ. It was not as much about the physical aspect for Jesus had already endured the scourging, a precursor to crucifixion. This was a calculated and targeted tactic to further subvert and punish their victim by attacking the essence of who he was and what he stood for.

With the "weight of the world" on his shoulders, Jesus sought the will of his Father, God. God, in turn, blessed his journey and sent him gifts to endure the trial. Jesus teaches us therefore, by his example, how to overcome the mental attacks that wound so deeply. Did Our Savior not possess every gift of the Holy Spirit from the cross? Certainly he did, and God has offered those same gifts to each of us.

When we are the ones being victimized he wants us to feel his presence. He desires to give hope to the spiritually lost while administering holy salve to the mentally wounded. He can soothe our sorrow and restore our dignity when we follow him.

Jesus also teaches us about humility even through the toughest mental abuse. The wounds of persecution and loneliness may be deep but he can help us forgive as he forgave. He can help us build back what has been destroyed. He can remove any pride that keeps us from obtaining peace, for his peace is pure and just.

The *Catechism of the Catholic Church* speaks about the value of our uniquely created souls and refers to Jesus as the "physician of our souls." It is a most fitting title.

Catholic Link

Catechism of the Catholic Church

363 In Sacred Scripture the term "soul" often refers to human *life* or the entire human *person*.[230] But "soul" also refers to the innermost aspect of man, that which is of greatest value in him,[231] that by which he is most especially in God's image: "soul" signifies the *spiritual principle* in man. **1421** The Lord Jesus Christ, physician of our souls and bodies, who forgave the sins of the paralytic and restored him to bodily health,[2] has willed that his Church continue, in the power of the Holy Spirit, his work of healing and salvation, even among her own members. This is the purpose of the two sacraments of healing: the sacrament of Penance and the sacrament of Anointing of the Sick.

[230] Cf. *Mt* 16:25-26; *Jn* 15:13; *Acts* 2:41. [231] Cf. *Mt* 10:28; 26:38; *Jn* 12:27; *2 Macc* 6:30.
[2] Cf. *Mk* 2:1-12. [231] Cf. *Mt* 10:28; 26:38; *Jn* 12:27; *2 Macc* 6:30.

The exact way God communicates with us, reaches out to us and teaches us is unknown to man. He uses hidden pathways known only to the Great Architect and Creator of body and soul. The instruction is wise and the path well lit. It quenches a thirst and satisfies a hunger we did not know we had. It pulls at us in a most comforting way as if we were toddlers being raised from our crib, Three Wise Men in pursuit of a star or martyrs who have seen the glory of God. It draws us to Him as if our souls were life's compasses and God the magnetic pull toward home.

THE LIGHT IS BLINDING ME

> *For everyone who does wicked things hates the light and does not come toward the light, so that his works might not be exposed. But whoever lives the truth comes to the light, so that his works may be clearly seen as done in God. John 3:20-21*

Oh, that our pure souls should be so close to God for His light to glow that brightly. It is not the bright light but rather the darkness that keeps us in a state of blindness.

Acclaimed journalist and producer Mike Leonard (note 4-2) spoke at our church during the rollout of the book and film *Catholicism, A journey to the heart of the faith.* He spoke of how his own faith deepened as he extensively traveled the globe with the author, Fr. Robert Barron. That evening he told us of the holy places he visited and the prayerful people he met. He told of stories of conversion and hope. At one point during the evening, he painted a visual picture of conversion that has remained imbedded in my mind. Here is the essence of what he said:

Our souls, like a car's windshield traveling fast into the night, gather the bugs, splashes and dust of everyday life in a sinner's world. We can drive all night and not notice the mess. One car's on-coming headlights may cause us to pause as they flash for us a glimpse of the truth upon our windshield. Several more may confirm the problem. But it is not until we turn our direction into the permanent light of God, allowing His truth to glisten upon the glass, that we truly see the muddle we have collected and the extent of the blindness we have endured.

Repentance through our Savior, like a hot and soapy car wash, cleanses away our sins and brings us anew. Even one tiny splash upon a clean windshield stands out, and we are eager to wipe it clean. The Light never lies to us nor does it hold hostage those who enter. We stay because we know the Light is true and the Light is good.

DISCUSSION CORNER

Describe, in your own words, Mike's analogy of the car's windshield as it compares to your journey. If the windshield represents your unique soul then what are the bugs, dust and dirt? Who in your life represents the on-coming headlights, which by their beaming example alone provide us an avenue of self-evaluation? Lastly, when our windshield accumulates dirt so too do the headlights. How does our own light dim to others when we do not regularly cleanse away the dirt?

Using the following quote from Edith Wharton, discuss what you think she meant by the two ways we can spread light. Discuss God's need for both candles and mirrors as we spread His light to others.

> *"There are two ways of spreading light; to be the candle, or the mirror that reflects it."*
>
> *Edith Wharton*

THE SACRAMENTS OF HEALING (AKA, DIRT REMOVAL)

Within the Catholic Church there are two sacraments of healing. They are the sacrament of Penance and the sacrament of Anointing of the Sick. The former sacrament is extensively used for purification throughout one's life; the other is used more sparingly for illness, suffering or when the possibility for death exists.

Jesus knew we would sin. He also knew we would feel remorse. Throughout his ministry, Jesus taught forgiveness and healed the contrite. In fact, many scripture passages reveal the compassion of Jesus upon his infirm followers. He healed them physically and he healed them spiritually. He healed them by touch and he healed them through being touched. But no matter how they were healed, Jesus felt compassion for them and cleared the way for them again to see the light.

Let's take a look at one of his more controversial healings. Please turn to and read the story of the paralytic found in Mark 2:1-12.

Exemplary is the faith of not only of the paralytic, but also the four men who carried him to Jesus. They believed so firmly in his power they did not let anything get in their way—not a crowd, not a blocked doorway and not even a roof. And Jesus' reaction was to show them deep compassion for their tenacity and ingenuity. There is a lesson here.

Also, I thought it quite interesting that Jesus chose to forgive the paralytic's sins before he healed his body (verse 5). And it was the forgiveness of sins that stirs the crowd into protest. Hmmm? Jesus takes the opportunity to question the scribes about their doubt in him by asking whether it is easier to heal spiritually or physically.

Why did Jesus choose to heal the man's sins first? We might never know what Jesus understood as the paralytic was being lowered in front of him. Perhaps the man felt himself unworthy of forgiveness yet his friends believed him worthy of a miracle. Perhaps it was a deep-seeded bitterness in his heart for the life he was given. Perhaps it was a more recent sin presenting an obstacle to accepting a physical healing from Jesus. Whatever it was, it was important to Jesus that it be cleared away first.

Can you imagine lying on a mat and being lowered by friends into a house where Jesus stands? You fully realize he has the power to make you walk but you secretly know your problems run deeper. You hope this little maneuver does not backfire as you swing side to side above the master's head, filling the only space not occupied by the throng of people. To your amazement, Jesus correctly diagnoses and clears your problem. Relief fills you as he heals your heart, cleanses your soul and forgives you for that which holds you captive. You rightfully wonder how he knew where to find the pain. Then, as if that were not enough, he heals your body too.

What would your answer have been if Jesus asked you which healing was easier: the cleansing of a soul or the physical healing of a body? He asked the scribes, so I pose the question to you for thought.

Maybe you have surmised it is easier to forgive sins because it does not require a medical miracle. After all, we even have the ability to forgive someone when they have wronged us so forgiveness may seem pretty easy. Also, you may recall when the apostles struggled with physical healings and Jesus was needed to save the day. So, possibly, it might be more difficult to make a paralyzed man walk than to forgive his sins.

What about the price tag God chose to place on forgiving our sins and cleansing our souls? That changes things, doesn't it? We cannot gloss over its incalculable value. A man named Jesus paid the hefty tab in full upon the cross. That kind of forgiveness is beyond our understanding as is the power to miraculously heal a body. Do you wonder if the only time it is difficult for God to perform a miracle is when our own faith is too weak to accept it? Therefore, we may have to chalk this question up under the category of "Messianic trick questions." Neither is even possible for us but our awesome God can do both!

Getting back to the two Catholic sacraments of healing, we see Jesus initiated them within his ministry and entrusted them to his Church that all of us might feel his extraordinary healing touch no matter what century we live in. It is no wonder that those who seek these sacraments speak of them as life changing, peace-filled and cleansing. Reconciliation offers us Jesus' healing touch through our priest. The same miracle experienced by the paralytic is experienced by the person confessing through the priest and is being delivered by the grace of Father, Son and Holy Spirit.

Some may ask why confession is necessary when God can choose to forgive sins not brought to him through a sacrament. It is true that God can forgive whenever and whomever he chooses. We have to believe God the Father was still allowing miracles in other towns and countries while God the Son walked this earth. Could then, the paralytic have said that the lines were too long and asked for God's healing from outside the house? Maybe, but he chose to go in because he wanted to be near Jesus. His faith told him to seek the guarantee and to do anything necessary to get there. He wanted to hear the words of forgiveness, feel the touch of healing and know without a doubt that the grace of God was ever-present. We are given the same amazing opportunity to see, hear and talk to the one given authority to channel forgiveness. Then we will know, with absolutely no doubt, we also have been forgiven.

Read the Catholic link below, which confers to the scripture passages of John 20:23 and 2 Corinthians 5:18, to understand the gift instituted by and handed down through Jesus to his beloved Church that we might experience the miracle of complete forgiveness. Note: It was difficult to choose only one excerpt as so much is written about this important sacrament. If you have the time please study this further *CCC 1420-1498.*

Catholic Link

Catechism of the Catholic Church

1461 Since Christ entrusted to his apostles the ministry of reconciliation, [65] bishops who are their successors, and priests, the bishops' collaborators, continue to exercise this ministry. Indeed bishops and priests, by virtue of the sacrament of Holy Orders, have the power to forgive all sins "in the name of the Father, and of the Son, and of the Holy Spirit."

[65] Cf. *Jn 20:23; 2 Cor 5:18.*

DISCUSSION CORNER

The crown of thorns was a "personal" attack on Jesus. We have both felt and inflicted such "personal" pain. Please take a few moments to write two prayers. The first should be a prayer of need, asking Jesus to help us deal with the bitterness of a deep wound. Allow yourself to be guided as you lay it down before him. Tell him how it hurt and how it helps you understand the pain he endured for us. If you need to still forgive the perpetrator please let His strength embrace and guide you.

The next should be a prayer asking forgiveness. Think about the people we may have intentionally or unintentionally wounded and the way our actions may have needlessly saddened their day, week or perhaps altered their life.

Before you finish, look at the first prayer you wrote asking for Jesus to help you. Did you remember to forgive your trespassers in the same manner you asked to be forgiven? You may be quick to forgive yet slow to feel worthy of forgiveness. You may be the opposite, slow to forgive yet quick to feel worthy of forgiveness. Analyze your thoughts while searching for a healthy balance between forgiving others and being forgiven.

Discuss what you can about the experience of writing down your needs. Describe how you felt and what you heard through opening yourself up to healing and forgiveness. Some of you may wish to share your prayers with the others. In which case, your group will receive a blessing.

LET THE CHILDREN COME

> . . . *"Let the children come to me; do not prevent them, for the kingdom of God belongs to such as these. Amen, I say to you, whoever does not accept the kingdom of God like a child will not enter it." Mark 10:14-15*

The disciples were trying to keep the children away from Jesus so they wouldn't bother his "adult" work. Jesus became annoyed with his disciples' lack of understanding, for he wanted the children near him. From the "mouth of babes" comes our next story.

A True Story . . .

It was the night before Easter and I found myself trying to explain a rather difficult concept to my two young daughters. The past Christmas was still fresh in their minds having occurred only a few months earlier. Keeping with the holiday tradition of Santa, they wanted to know if they should be putting cookies and milk out for the Easter Bunny as well. *How cute!* I thought it the perfect segue to discuss the real meaning of Easter and attempted to bridge the gap of baby Jesus to sacrificed Savior. It was a tall order for two young minds to grasp and so as I finished I asked if they had any questions. They murmured a "no" and went on their way. I thought to myself: *they did not understand a word you just said. All they wanted to know was whether or not to leave cookies and milk out. Why the long explanation?*

About thirty minutes later, my answer was delivered. Our two girls ran back into the family room where my husband and I were watching television. They had excitement in their voices and goodies in their hands. "Mom," they shouted, "we have something the Easter Bunny can give to Jesus." *Okay, this should be good!*

Instead of milk and cookies they decided to give the thirsting Jesus a glass of sparkling cool water. They told me vinegar was mean and the soldiers should not have done that to Jesus. They then held out a few of their favorite neon colored adhesive bandages claiming they were for the sores on his head. I was impressed.

Then, in utter amazement, my eyes focused on their next gift. It was a simple crown made from construction paper. The bright colors of crayon drawings made it happy and cheerful. And then they asked, "Did you see inside the crown, mom?" I craned my neck to get a better look at the crown they held so tightly in their tiny, glue-sticky fingers. And there they were—a small handful of cotton balls stuck to the inside of the crown, strategically placed to soften the weight when placed against a tender head. Our Savior's head, that is.

I could not believe my eyes or my ears. No wonder Jesus loved the children so very much. No wonder he called them to him even when he was tired—possibly especially when he was tired—of adults, that is! They were his comfort because they believed so completely in who he was. They understood more through their innocence than we do through our experience. They possess the effortless faith that we, as adults, now must purposefully seek.

Our daughters each had one last thing to offer Jesus. Hidden behind their backs, but now in full view, came each girl's most favored stuffed animal. Not one of the new ones they hardly played with but the one they could not go to sleep without. A little puzzled, I asked why they chose this gift for Jesus. With one of those tilted head smiles, as if I should have already known, they said, "hugging it would make him feel all-better."

I proudly left each gift out that night for the Easter Bunny to see. What an amazing gift of gratitude from the heart. What an amazing lesson to teach the adults in the household! There on the coffee table lay the gifts of blind faith and true compassion. On the evening before the great celebration of our Christ resurrected, they gave him the best they had to offer. In those acts he will always find comfort. Let the children come!

RIGHT KING, WRONG CROWN

The "crowning of thorns" meditation both heals the persecuted and stirs contrition in the unjust, allowing each of us to visualize where we would have stood in the cohort of soldiers surrounding Jesus. We may not be able to envision ourselves crucifying Jesus, but the crown of thorns engages each one of us. It forces us to recognize even our slightest sins against our fellow brothers and sisters as we humbly ask for forgiveness.

And so we pray . . .

Dear Jesus, how did they not know the rightful king stood before them? How did they not see through your humility that you are the Son of Man? Oh, honorable and righteous Lord Jesus, you are to be adored. Allow our adoration, reverence, and glory to create for you a new crown. This time let it be woven with our love instead of hatred, charity instead of cruelty, compassion instead of indifference and understanding instead of reprisal.

We implore you to use the strength of our faith to transform the dinginess of a woven branch to the luster of a golden crown. We ask that our reverence be used to soften the spikes of scorn. Allow our repentance to serve the crown, keeping its brightness bold through our cleansed and purified souls.

Help us, dear God, to serve Your beloved Son who in turn serves You. May the Holy Spirit keep the crown ever before us and lead us back to You. In the precious name of Jesus, we pray.

Fourth Prayer: The Crowning of Thorns

The prayer of St. Bridget for the Crowning of Thorns

Pray 1 Our Father, 1 Hail Mary, then:

Eternal Father, through Mary's unblemished hands and the Divine Heart of Jesus, I offer You the Wounds, the Pains, and the Precious Blood of Jesus' Holy Head from the Crowning with Thorns as atonement for my and all of humanity's sins of the Spirit, as protection against such sins and the spreading of Christ's kingdom here on earth.

The Carrying of the Cross

Bible passages needed for study of this chapter:

John 19:16-17	1 Peter 2:15-17	John 15:15-17
2 Peter 2:19	1 Peter 2:21-25	John 8:31-45

Please read John 19:16-17

It is interesting to note John's gospel is the only one to profess Jesus carrying his own cross. The others identify Simon the Cyrenian as the one who carried the cross of Jesus. It is uncertain how long Jesus was able to endure the weight before Simon was called to help him but we can surmise that if Jesus had the strength to carry it for the entire stretch, and at the pace the Roman soldiers required, Jesus would have been required to do it himself.

Some believe it was the grace of God alone that sustained Jesus through this walk to Golgotha; the severe beatings alone could have caused him to drop dead. It was God's will, and therefore the will of His Only Begotten Son, to make it to the cross. God allowed his prolonged agony for our salvation. The tremendous courage of Jesus to finish this excruciatingly painful job of sin-rectification left no human sin uncovered. He gathered the venial sins upon the cross and it was heavy. Then he added the weight of our mortal sins and it was unbearable. It proves the depth and breadth of his forgiveness and the unfathomable love he has for us.

TRY TO MAKE ME

A True Story . . .

After about a year of contemplating on my own these times Jesus shed blood for us, I began interviewing friends about them. I would state each of the seven titles without commentary and then ask which one stirs the most emotion or seems to be the most difficult for them to follow. I was looking for depth in their thoughts that might aid me in my research and understanding.

The majority of them stated the "Crucifixion" as the most troubling. Easy for us to understand, it was a barbaric and gruesome practice of torture no longer used for even the worst criminals. A few stated the "Agony in the Garden" stirred sorrow in them and they helped me see the torment Christ suffered over the sins of the world. One dear friend chose "The Carrying of the Cross." Puzzled to hear the unexpected choice, I looked up from where I was taking notes to see her tearing up. Then she explained:

"All the others were done to him, as a victim, but picking up the cross was voluntary. This is where I would have called it quits."

She went on to explain her wrestling with the emotion of picking up a cross, carrying it through the streets along side the convicted rebels and being looked upon with such disdain and evil-induced gratification. These thoughts were beyond her comprehension. If she had been required to do the same she would have chosen to sit it out . . . literally, she said, she would have sat on the ground and given them permission to beat her to death there.

Her thoughts wondered as she tried to piece it together: *Why pick up the cross that prolonged the agony, furthered the abuse and re-stimulated the humiliation? Why feed the egotistical monster? Why give satisfaction to the unjust? After all, it would be like admitting guilt to those you knew were guilty.*

And yet that is exactly what our humble Christ Jesus did for us in this blood-shedding moment. He **chose** to pick up the cross because he **chose** to pick up our sins. In a way he was guilty because he claimed our guilt for himself. Her heartfelt analysis helped me realize the extent Christ absorbed the burden of our sinfulness and the choices he made along the way to embrace, rather than simply fulfill, his earthly mission.

She also made an excellent point about human nature and the defenses we post to prove a point. Humiliation is something all of us try to avoid, especially when we are innocent.

At the end of her explanation came an unexpected puzzle piece, but one that fit perfectly into the landscape she had drawn. Attempting to hold back the tears she spoke of a time she had been held at gunpoint while a stranger entered her car. With gun pointed toward her head, he commanded the route she was forced to drive. So many dreadful thoughts and fears resurfaced as she explained the day in detail.

No one will ever find me. One hour passed, then two, as many miles of road separated her from the town she knew and the people she loved. There was no mistaking his intentions as he boldly intimidated her. His shameless actions and violent descriptions foretold an unpleasant ending to the nightmare as it unfolded before her. She was not his first victim. She would not be his last.

Does anybody care? She attempted subtle, yet desperate, pleas to any fellow driver within range of seeing her yet wondered how not one noticed her apparent distress. An uncomfortable and sad isolation enveloped her as car, after car, after car went passing by. By this time it was getting late and the safety of daylight was sinking into the horizon. So too her hopes were fading as she knew darkness left her no advantage against him.

Try to make me. Refusing to submit to his sick pleasure, she silently prayed to the only One who could save her. She decided that she would no longer help this vile man orchestrate her demise. She would not drive herself any further away. And she would not keep "hoping" when hope was never going to come. So she drew the line that determined her fate. The plan was risky but she had nothing to lose.

At the very next exit ramp she steered the car off the highway . . . came to a dead stop . . . and firmly informed her tormentor she was no longer his driver. As you can imagine, he didn't take the news very well. He was furious at her boldness toward him and tried to use the gun and force to help her change her mind. She remained totally and confidently resolute.

After a string of failed attempts on his part to get the car moving again, she presumed he intended to take over the driving. She did not wait around to see. As soon as the passenger door opened and both his feet hit the pavement, hers hit the gas. And the bullet he fired off thankfully did not reach her.

Within minutes back on the interstate she spotted her solace just ahead. Determined but full of fear, she vowed not to allow this chance at hope to disappear. Trembling, she punched the gas and floored it . . . until she smashed the front of her car into the fender of a police car. Someone finally noticed her!

Each person has a story where God gave us the necessary courage, grace, and wisdom to 1) stay the course peacefully, 2) fight the necessary battle, or 3) spare us through a back door. Hopefully not many of you have dealt with the intense fear and anxiety my friend underwent but she would be the first to admit Jesus was the one who spared her life that day.

My friend has used her zest for living and passion for Jesus to serve as magnets bringing others closer to the one who spared her life. Many people are grateful for her and the many blessings she has chosen to pay forward. She is one of those people who changes lives through her example and her ministry, normally tens or hundreds at a time. She is an amazing woman!

I often wonder, knowing the kind of person she is, if it was the thought of others falling victim to him after her that raised the level of her determination and resolve. She may have decided to "sit this one out" (so to speak) by not going along with his sick scheme, but she did not quit. She followed Jesus down a different path and her bravery and trust in God threw a huge wrench in the monster's normal chain of events. She was willing to gamble with her life for the chance to stop him. Perhaps her boldness frightened him into never trying it again. Perhaps he eventually sought help after "the girl with the courage to stand up to him" shook his evil-driven confidence. We do not know what happened to the vile and sick person who was left on the road that day, but we know where Jesus and his angels were as they tended to the one God loves— they were helping her navigate a most dreadful and frightful storm.

It is important for us to study the hardships suffered by Jesus because we cannot "do" this life without him. Our world is full of free wills and not all of those wills follow God. Following Jesus is the only way to battle evil, as he will walk ahead of us to show us the route to take. Every circumstance requires a path all its own and Jesus knows the way. He forged the path to Calvary so we might trust him to lead us. Following him makes even the hardest roads navigable.

DISCUSSION CORNER

Take time to discuss your story of God-given courage, grace, and wisdom. Think about the three ways (outlined above) God used to help you navigate a situation. Are there additional ways God has aided you not mentioned above? Has He used a combination of these over a period of time?

Which blood shedding moment speaks uniquely to you? Why? Is Jesus teaching you about his sacrifice through your experiences?

FREEDOM AND CHOICES

God grants us the freedom to choose. Every day we make choices for or against evil and likewise for or against God. When God showers us with blessings, illuminates the path of His will or uses grace to comfort the contrite, is He unfairly bribing us to choose in His favor? If so, does He then manipulate our freedom?

You may never have given this question consideration yet many over the years have pondered it. Perhaps you believe it unfaithful to question God's intentions and simply leave it at that. Others may claim that we can never stump the Almighty, so everything is fair game. Does a fine line exist between asking Him and doubting Him?

He was the one who gave us the brain to think and voice to debate so perhaps He encourages us to challenge, especially when the questions force us to spend time getting to know Him. The more time we devote to Him, even if it is to try to disprove Him, the more time He has to be close to us. And He is all for that!

There are many wonderful books written by former non-believers who fell in love with God after researching Him. Their attempts to once-and-for-all slam the door on God were exactly what drove them directly to His almighty lap and led them through a doorway to an inner peace they never knew existed. God can work with our passions even when they are first targeted in opposition to Him.

The books written by converts to Catholicism add even another dimension to the richness of our faith. They remind cradle Catholics to never take for granted the gift of our Holy and Apostolic Church, instituted by Jesus Christ. They speak with enthusiasm about the early church fathers and saints whose wisdom and sacrifice blazed trails for future generations. They honor each sacrament, and you can feel their excitement and hope. The new Catholics have been filled-up with the Holy Spirit and they gladly radiate Him from head to toe. They bless our churches with a fire and zeal so contagious, even tired veterans feel re-energized.

No matter how many times God is "re-discovered," each human's experience is a unique and personal discovery. It is as if our treasure lay dormant within each of our souls, safely hidden for the Master Locksmith to open. His patience over time, like the tumblers of a safe falling slowly into place, opens the door to a sacred place inside us. The place only He can find, only He can open and only He can fill—when we allow Him.

There is an undeniable tenderness existing between God and His creations that might have been overlooked had someone not had the audacity to first ask the "freedom and choices" question. Let us now look to scripture for insight and knowledge.

Do we really have a choice? Read 2 Peter 2:19.

This passage claims we are slaves to whatever overcomes us, be it evil or good. There is no middle ground here yet the choice remains ours to make.

Are there rules to freedom? Flip back one book to Read 1 Peter 2:15-17.

Our obedience to the will of God can be used to hush the "ignorant talk of foolish men". Awesome! But we must be careful how we use this freedom. Following these rules (verse 17) will help.

What is our universal calling and why? Please now read the passage of 1 Peter 2:21-25.

Verse 21 states the calling and verses 24-25 reveal how Jesus' suffering was necessary to free us so we might hear our calling. The "guardian of our souls," in verse 25, describes a special bond and intimacy that should make us feel honored and loved. No wonder the shepherd had a vested interest in his sheep, for He was protecting not only our lives but also our eternal souls.

What relationship developed for the apostles who chose to follow Christ's footsteps and the new command? Read John 15:15-17.

These imperfect and simple men went from *slave* to *friend* when they chose to accompany Jesus. What a promotion! The Bible footnotes also explain the significance of this development from Old Testament times. While Moses, Joshua and David remained "servants" or "slaves" of God, only Abraham was ever proclaimed a "friend of God." Through Jesus, our relationship with God transforms.

This next exchange may turn some lights on for you. Slavery is the prerequisite to freedom through Christ. Slavery is also the prerequisite to hell. Read John 8:31-45.

Jesus spoke to the Jews who wanted to kill him, using truth to dissuade them, yet their hardheaded behavior held them back from God. We either buy into the lies or we buy into the truth, but the cost is the same: submission. The difference, however, comes after submitting:

- Evil holds us as a prisoner. Guilt and shame are the bars and blocked walls that contain our sins. One sin notoriously begets more sins as easily as one lie creates a need for more (and bigger) lies. Think of the way you feel after sinning against someone you care about. Does that feeling have anything to do with freedom?
- God holds us up as heirs to His heavenly eternity. Submitting is recognizing Him as our Father and us His children. He created us to love Him and therefore He knows what fulfills us. Through Christ we are free because Christ is the Truth. Read verse 35 and 36 again. Jesus distinguishes a slave from a child of the Master. Because he is the Son of the Master he has the authority to free us . . . from sin, from bondage and from evil. He uses that authority to bring us in as co-heirs by redeeming us and making us worthy.

So you are no longer a slave but a child, and if a child then also an heir, through God. Galatians 4: 7

In conclusion: God emboldens us in a similar manner to the way loving parents encourage their own children. Submitting to the laws of the house allow children privileges and freedoms as they mature. Those rules also keep them safe and on track.

Because of the limitless resources God has at His disposal, you might consider His tactics a bit manipulative. He loves us that much—to use anything to get our attention. No matter our age we are still young children in the eyes of God, needing guidance and instruction to navigate the waters of naïveté. The world is full of monsters and the safest place we can position ourselves is behind the shield of Christ, guardian of our souls.

And the teachings of the church:

Catholic Link

Catechism of the Catholic Church

1742 *Freedom and grace.* The grace of Christ is not in the slightest way a rival of our freedom when this freedom accords with the sense of the true and the good that God has put in the human heart. On the contrary, as Christian experience attests especially in prayer, the more docile we are to the promptings of grace, the more we grow in inner freedom and confidence during trials, such as those we face in the pressures and constraints of the outer world.

HUMBLE SERVANT

Choosing to pick up the cross for us was one of many acts of humility Jesus performed throughout his life. If you had to describe Jesus to someone you might choose words like Savior, teacher or healer. You might admit he was empathetic, loving and compassionate, yet radical, disciplined and profound. He was both simple and complex, hard yet soft. Deep in the simplicity of the humble Son-made-Man was a complex God who chose to demonstrate His love rather than dictate it. Love became the new commandment and it all started with Jesus.

> *I give you a new commandment: love one another. As I have loved you, so you also should love one another. John 13:34*

Jesus commands us to love one another. That sounds easy enough until he uses himself as the example of *how* to love one another. Ouch, he is no easy act to follow! He loved every one of us so completely, withholding nothing and giving everything.

Jesus teaches us how to love through his example on the cross, forgiving his persecutors just as he forgives us when we sin against him. That too is our directive. As our slavery withers to a solid friendship with Jesus, so to does our responsibility grow to love one another like he did. We are called to the standard Jesus set for us and measured by our willingness to obey the command.

It truly is as simple as that. The rule is not complicated. It does not contain asterisks or options. It is the straightforwardness that causes us to doubt. *But what about . . . or if this happens, then can I . . . ?* Did such questions enter into the mind of Jesus as he picked up the cross for us? If so he immediately dismissed them. I doubt such excuses were penetrable to a man who loved us so perfectly, sheltered us so closely and desired our love so emphatically. It all funnels back to the same thing:

> Our Lord loved us first, so we would know how to love.
> Our Lord forgave us first, so we would know how to forgive.
> We are called to follow in the footsteps of Our Lord.

Read the Catholic Link below for further insight into our calling. Pay close attention to the last sentence, it is a doozy!

Catholic Link

Catechism of the Catholic Church

1878 All men are called to the same end: God himself. There is a certain resemblance between the unity of the divine persons and the fraternity that men are to establish among themselves in truth and love. [1] Love of neighbor is inseparable from love for God.

[1] Cf. *GS* 24 § 3.

THE SILENT PARTNERS

As stated in the beginning of this chapter, Simon the Cyrenian was credited for helping Jesus carry his cross in the gospels of Matthew, Mark and Luke. The passages explain Simon was "pressed into service" to carry the cross of Jesus. In other words, Jesus was in need and he responded—possibly forced, but nonetheless Simon delivered. Without Simon, you could say, Jesus may not have made it to the crucifixion atop Calvary.

This passage paints a picture for us that could easily be overlooked if we do not pay close attention. The Roman soldiers would have happily beaten Jesus more to move him along had the issue been defiance. They witnessed his willingness to make the journey, yet he struggled. The divinity of Jesus embraced a cross his humanness could no longer carry. Jesus' heart was engaged and willing but his body was weak and failing. The soldiers had one mission and it was to get him to the top of the hill for crucifixion. (Perhaps they did not realize from "whom" the directive truly came!) Either way, they made the necessary provisions by invoking a strong and capable assistant to help Jesus carry the cross.

What if Simon had refused, pleaded for vindication, or been absent when Jesus came by? Would God have chosen someone else to be "pressed into service" or would He have chosen to allow Jesus to perish on the road to the cross? Simon may not have been too excited about the job he was asked to do, but what a remarkable piece of history he made that afternoon . . . because God's will, not his, was fulfilled.

> *As they led him away they took hold of a certain Simon, a Cyrenian, who was coming in from the country; and after laying the cross on him, they made him carry it behind Jesus. Luke 23:26*

God still recruits the "Simons" of the world. Jesus still needs them to pick up the slack and to keep his journey alive for future generations. All across the globe today and throughout time, Jesus has chosen his silent partners to help carry crosses. If we pitch in on the heavy lifting he will do the rest. Please notice in the scripture above where Jesus was in relation to Simon for this particular journey.

Jesus did not follow behind Simon and he did not choose to walk beside him. Instead, Jesus walked ahead of him. Jesus led Simon, as he still leads us today, on the road to salvation.

DISCUSSION CORNER

Jesus was required to accept the help of Simon. What do you think went through his mind?

- I'd really rather do it myself
- Concerned the credit would now have to be shared
- Grateful, but a bit annoyed inside
- Consumed with fear or concern for the person "pressed into service"
- Fully accepting, heartened and encouraged
- An opportunity to bless the one sent to bless him (Reciprocal blessings!)
- Thankful for the answer to a prayer for help
- Other

Some of these choices sound ridiculous when considering it is Jesus we are speaking about, but now try to truthfully examine a time you were required to accept help. (Perhaps when you lacked enough experience to do it on your own, were ill, recovering from an accident or surgery, or needed assistance because of age.) Do the options still sound ridiculous? Discuss the options above and any you added. What kind of humility, rewards and blessings are inherent in being a Simon for Christ?

A GOOD FIGHT

All of this talk about humility has me wondering about the times the cross requires us to fight. Do you think a conflict of interest exists when

Christians are asked to both submit . . . and also fight; show peace . . . yet retaliate? In other words, we are asked to pick up the cross . . . then use it to wallop someone!

Jesus handled it this way. He taught peace yet he defended his Father's house. He spoke tolerance for others, yet rebuked their faithless ways. He forgave, yet he held his followers accountable. It is a balancing act we practice our entire lives and possibly will never perfect like Jesus did but fighting for peace is what some of us will be called to do.

1 Maccabees is about such a conflict. A fascinating story in itself, it tells of a time when the devout Jewish people refused the king's command to forsake God's laws and commandments. In fear, they fled from their homes leaving all their possessions behind. The king's men followed them out with orders to kill them.

The fleeing Jewish families, because of one huge flaw in their plan, were dying rapidly at the hand of the Gentiles' army. They refused to fight, retaliate, guard themselves or cast a single stone . . . on the Sabbath. It didn't take long for the enemy to figure out the highly effective strategy of using the holy day of rest as their guarantee for victory.

Then came a righteous leader named Mattathias and his five sons who realized fighting was part of the cross they were asked to bear. Read the words of Mattathias after one of the holy day plunders:

> *When Mattathias and his friends heard of it, they mourned deeply for them. They said to one another, "If we all do as our kindred have done, and do not fight against the Gentiles for our lives and our laws, they will soon destroy us from the earth." So on that day they came to this decision: "Let us fight against anyone who attacks us on the sabbath, so that we may not all die as our kindred died in their secret refuges." 1 Maccabees 2:39-41*

Evil does not sleep—and, evidently, neither does it observe holy days. Evil preys on the kind-hearted, hoping their patience outlasts their ruination. Evil looks for the one who turns the other cheek, offers no resistance and hands over their cloak when they have been robbed of their tunic. (cf.

Matthew 5:39-41) Jesus demands his followers to love and to follow the commandments of God yet God does not wish for his people to perish from the face of the Earth. How, then, do we make sense of God's will?

The Catechism of the Catholic Church speaks of this very dilemma. It is too in depth to do it justice with a snippet here, so I will direct you to its words of wisdom and recap some of the teachings. (CCC Safeguarding Peace, #2302-2330)

First and foremost, it speaks of the Fifth Commandment forbidding the intentional destruction of human life and asks each of us to pray that God will free us from the bondage of war. With that said, it speaks about defending our countries from evil in order for common good to prevail. It speaks about honorable duties of peacekeepers and those who are charged with the maintenance of peace.

It speaks of how Jesus teaches us humility while refraining from retaliation because he knows our hearts and he knows that anger can provoke a rash of unequalled counterattacks. That, in turn, can breed decades of retaliation, until the subject that first caused the dispute is no longer even remembered. The fight now belongs solely to the last retaliation and it never ends.

He teaches us to keep a calm head as we keep true to loving our neighbor. A calm-headed discipline of morals coupled with just punishment is sometimes required. Every person must be held accountable to the rules if peace is to be a reality . . . in our homes, in our towns, in our countries and in our world.

THE EASY WAY

A True Story . . .

I received a cartoon-type email a long time ago that had stick figures walking from left to right across the page. Each figure carried a huge cross upon their back. In the next frame, you could see all of the figures beginning to sweat, as the burdens got heavier and the trail more rugged.

One of the stick figures pulled out a saw and started hacking away at the cross he was to carry. Leaving a hunk of his cross on the ground behind him he resumed his journey. A few frames later, while others continued to slow down and some fell under the weight of their crosses, the stick figure with the already shortened cross stopped again . . . long enough to saw a few more feet off the cross he carried. With only a few feet of cross left, he handily tucked it under his arm and began running past all of the others.

At this point, I began to wonder about the crux of this email. I was actually getting annoyed with the one who kept cheating because it made him look like the only smart one in the bunch. Why portray him in such a good light? Others were struggling, falling, and crying. Some were trying to help carry part of another's' cross along with their own. He skipped along, fresh as a daisy, while the others looked sad and desperate. If it had not been for the credibility of the person who sent this email to me, I would have closed the scene before the last of the frames popped into view. I am glad I waited.

In the last scene there was a chasm. I watched as the figures approached the bottomless pit and wondered what they would do now. Confidently they approached the chasm. That is, except the one who had cheated. Those with their full-length crosses in tow raised them at the edge of the chasm and allowed them to fall into place against the opposite side. The full burden of the cross they had carried created the perfectly sized bridge. Once in place the stick figure walked safely from one side to the other. The one who cheated . . . well he could not "cross" the chasm because he had no "cross" to offer.

The cartoon redeemed itself in a way I had not foreseen and then it caused me to wonder . . . how many times have I whittled at my own cross? Do I sometimes mistake life for a race, assuming I am best if I am able to run ahead? Watching the stick figure do it I saw it clearly as cheating. Of course when I do it, it seems more like survival.

Is there a fine line we need to pay attention to? We can dress up our self-centered busyness, put it on a big stick and walk around with it all day long but it will never be a cross. In our attempts to "simplify" our lives, are we hacking away at the stick we chose to pick up—or the cross we were asked to bear?

Each of us has to determine when God is calling us and when the devil is trying to keep us too busy to answer. Whose will are we serving? How are we choosing to use our precious time on earth? Maybe our prayer should be simply to distinguish our true cross from our self-imposed burdens. The latter can certainly keep us busy but such burdens will hinder us from bearing fruit. Crosses, although manufactured on Earth (we will have no crosses in heaven), come with a heavenly guarantee to be fruitful and filled with grace.

THANK YOU, DEAR JESUS

Let us pray:

It is during this time of blood shedding, dear sweet Jesus, that we realize your individual love for us, for those were our sins adding to the weight upon your tender shoulder. If our sins were not there, we would not be forgiven. So, we know they were there.

They were there for each of us long before we uttered them, thought them or committed them. You knew our sins, judgments, and failings before we were even born. Knowing all you still chose to pick up the cross, carry it and allow our sins and your precious body to be nailed to the cross of redemption.

Allow us to be your Simons and to see your will above all else. We ask you now for the extra graces to get through the tough stuff, knowing that dependence on you is where we are most secure. Mark the spot clearly of exactly where you want us so that we might follow closely behind you. Let your shepherding voice be what we hear above all other voices. Help us find you and help us stay near you. Soften our hearts so completely that they yearn for you alone, for it is when our hearts are joined to you that we can find the happiness you want so desperately to share with us. Remind us, through our fears, that not a single place you could ask us to go is unknown to you first. In fact, you, dear Jesus, stand waiting for us still.

Fifth Prayer: The Carrying of the Cross

The prayer of St. Bridget for the Carrying of the Cross

Pray 1 Our Father, 1 Hail Mary, then:

Eternal Father, through Mary's unblemished hands and the Divine Heart of Jesus, I offer You the Sufferings on the way of the Cross, especially His Holy Wound on His Shoulder and its Precious Blood as atonement for my and all of humanity's rebellion against the Cross, every grumbling against Your Holy Arrangements and all other sins of the tongue, as protection against such sins and for true love of the Cross.

The Crucifixion

Bible passages needed for study of this chapter:

Mark 15:22-32	1 Corinthians 11: 23-26	Revelation 8:3-4
John 19:16-24	Luke 7: 6-10	Luke 23:39-43
Matthew 20:30-34	Revelation 16:17	
Mark 11: 9-10	Revelation 1:12-13	

Please read Mark 15:22-32 for our first gospel account.

These verses are heart wrenching. Please allow yourself to be present when you read this gospel accounting of the crucifixion of our Lord, Jesus. Read it several times if you wish while immersing yourself deeper into the story that never stops teaching us.

The sights and sounds of a sincere meditation can be overwhelming yet remarkably intuitive. Some may say they feel bitterness or a coldness surround them when they allow themselves to travel back in time to Our Lord's crucifixion. Others may be remorseful. Some may gain incredible perspective and renewed faith while still others may better understand the extent of his torment and pain. Some may even get a headache from the pounding of the nails and the involuntary moans of a man they love being crucified for the sins of mankind. Others may concentrate on the placard placed above his head and the crowd that relentlessly mocked him. Still others may cringe at the thoughtlessness of the soldiers who gamble in front of Jesus for the tunic he will no longer have need for.

Jesus touches each person who comes to him in a different way. He reveals to each of us an excruciating moment during his crucifixion that he dedicates to us, and to our suffering. He desires for us to know his love . . .

> *No one has greater love than this, to lay down one's life for one's friends. John 15:13*

DISCUSSION CORNER

In this chapter we are starting right off with discussion. The crucifixion personally speaks to each of us and it is important to reflect on and share your thoughts first. As a group, please pray to the Holy Spirit for insight and meaningful discussion. The following is a simple prayer often used by Catholics and proves highly effective for discernment. You may wish to try it, slowly repeating it a few times.

Come, Holy Spirit, fill the hearts of your faithful and enkindle in us the fire of your love.

As a group, have one person read the previous scripture aloud. Then have another read the account in John 19:16-24 for additional insight. Reflect accordingly while they are reading.

- o Imagine an aerial view of the scene. Build the scene in your mind like a movie director would in preparation for the shoot. Spy the soldiers, crowd and disciples. What is stirring Jerusalem on this day? Feel the developing dramatic undertow as this particular day and this particular crucifixion forever change history.
- o Listen as Pontius Pilate dictates the words of Jesus' crime and then firmly defends his statement. Why do you think Pilate had the courage to defend the title he gave to Jesus, but not Jesus himself? Do we sometimes make the same contradiction?
- o Slightly change focus by dropping yourself to ground level as you become one with the crowd surrounding Jesus. You observe those around you—the indifferent, the cold and the heartbroken. Now change your focus to look only for the face of Jesus upon the cross. Align your heart to his sighs, breathe when he breathes, hear what he hears, and see what he sees.
- o Discuss the sights, sounds, and emotions of the scene you were given. What did you perceive about him during his crucifixion? Did you feel peace or agony? Did you feel both or neither? What happened to your heart as you allowed his crucifixion to fill your thoughts? Share with each other your gift of personal perspective.

TURNING INTO THE PAIN

Generally speaking, when it comes to pain—most people try to avoid it. Some will argue it must be endured for as they say, "no pain, no gain." That pain is different. Think about the easily escapable pain that, for whatever reason, we allow to invade us. In fact, we turn ourselves into it. Why would you ever choose to not duck the blow when you clearly see the punch coming? Why run miles on a broken leg, climb a rope with bleeding hands or plunge yourself into icy waters, unless . . . it is the only path between you and saving the ones you love.

Jesus taught us this one from the cross.

Do you remember when we read the passage from Mark 15 at the beginning of this chapter? Verse 32 states that the criminals crucified with Jesus "also kept abusing him." *C'mon, really? For heaven's sake, don't criminals who die together, bind together?*

Having already endured physical, emotional and spiritual distress, Jesus had to be completely worn out. And the pain . . . had to be beyond unbearable. He lay upon his cross placed between two criminals who were chiming in on the hateful harassment. If this was not a breaking point for our Lord it's hard to imagine what would be. However, even through all of this, Jesus did not lose heart. One priest pointed out to me the correlation between Jesus crying out *"I thirst"* (John 19:28) and his thirst for converts, even from the cross.

During his ministry Jesus saved the Samaritan woman at the well by asking her to *"Give me a drink"* (John 4:7), and in turn blessed her with an internal spring of water for everlasting life. Jesus never stopped teaching us, never stopped loving us, never stopped healing us and never stopped thirsting for us . . . even moments before his brutal death.

Please read Luke 23:39-43, for the miracle of salvation for a criminal who opened his heart to the Great Teacher's last words.

Here is an image for you to ponder from the words you just read. Try to feel the compassion flow into the heart of Jesus as the formerly hateful criminal beside him was given the eyes to see, the ears to hear and the mouth to finally proclaim that innocent Jesus was indeed the Son of God. Such compassion would have a cost for a Savior. Does it not make sense to think Jesus would have genuinely tried to acknowledge the repentant criminal who would be the first to step-up to quench his thirst?

Even if he could not make direct eye contact, Jesus would have at least strained his body or turned his head to directly speak the words of forgiveness to the criminal beside him and to offer him an everlasting reward in the Kingdom of God. That kind of exchange would not have been half-heartedly spoken. It would not have been shouted into the air in hopes that the words would somehow find the ear they were meant for. No, Jesus would have targeted his words carefully and, in doing so, would have paid an excruciating price. For it is then we must recall the crown of thorns upon his tender head and the nails that bound his feet and hands. Yes, Jesus turned into the pain to acknowledge the repentant soul . . . because he knew it was the ONLY path to save the ones he loved.

Pray for the strength to endure your own path, to understand the timing of His perfect will and the ability to bring peace to those you meet along your way. All of us were created to both accept salvation and to lead others to it—even when the path means turning into the pain.

IMPORTANT LAST WORDS

If you were given the opportunity to make a statement prior to your death wouldn't you make the most of it? If you could choose your audience whom would you include and what would the message sound like?

If the sum of a person's life can be found in the words they choose to say near death then Jesus has a few additional lessons to teach us from the cross. It is only fair to mention first that Jesus was pretty chatty the night before his crucifixion. If you have a Bible where all of Jesus' words are typed in red, then you have the visual of what I am talking about. The chapters leading to the crucifixion are heavily laden in red ink as Jesus offers instruction, foretelling and hope.

With the twelve apostles still intact, Jesus taught multiple timeless lessons during the Last Supper and then again to the few who entered the Garden for prayer. Once Jesus' body was bound to the cross, his words became targeted yet universal, poignant yet full of hope. They truly are an amazing representation of when human meets divine at death's door.

Below are the seven remarks:

1. *"My God, my God, why have you forsaken me?* Found in both Matthew 27:46 and Mark 15:34
2. *"Father, forgive them, they know not what they do."* Luke 23:34
3. *"Amen, I say to you, today you will be with me in Paradise."* Luke 23:43
4. *"Father, into your hands I commend my spirit."* Luke 23:46
5. *"Woman, behold your son."* and *"Behold your mother."* John 19:26-27
6. *"I thirst."* John 19:28
7. *"It is finished."* John 19:29

A few of these statements (3 and 6) should sound familiar to you since we already studied them (Turning into the Pain). Let us review each of Jesus' declarations to the people standing watch:

1. *"My God, my God, why have you forsaken me?"* There are numerous explanations of this statement floating around, some of which are provided below:

   a) He alone could empty the cup of sins required for our salvation, therefore in his depths of giving he transcended into a place no human had gone before or will ever be able to go again. He, in his emptiness, was fully alone.

   b) Feeling forsaken by God, but remaining with God, is the ultimate test of our mandating His will above our will. We must trust the power of God working within us and allow selflessness to replace every selfish thought we have. Like the book of Job and many saints who have experienced darkness and solitude during their lives, God allows some of His strongest to feel complete emptiness. In simple form, He removes both the training wheels and his supportive hand from the bicycle we are riding. Like a parent who knows his child is ready, He hides in the window to watch (and silently cheer) as His holy children courageously perfect the balance He once controlled. When God so fully lives within His holy children and His children are ready to try it alone, the extra balancing hand and training wheels can actually hinder or slow progress. With trust and with great pride, He lets us go—but never stops monitoring our progress.

   c) Psalm 22. This Psalm has been linked to these verses found within Matthew and Mark and for good reason. Psalm 22 was an ancient hymn of suffering and praise known to the Jewish people. Jesus would have uttered the first line, as the others would have silently followed his lead. The verses in the hymn (broken into four parts, 2-12, 13-22, 23-27, 28-32), point to the fulfillment of Jesus upon the cross and to the salvation the Jewish people had long awaited.

2. *"Father, forgive them, they know not what they do."* Forgiveness. Oh, the many lessons we can find in this short but powerful request of Son to Father. Already beginning his reparation for our sins in the thick of his suffering, Jesus holds not one person accountable for his horrendous crucifixion. He now begs his Father to also pardon them, understanding and acknowledging the Father's intense love for his obedient son. This is a beautiful exchange as Jesus calms the anger of the Father he knows so well, all while reminding us to forgive our debtors as we hope to be forgiven of our sins.

3. *"Amen, I say to you, today you will be with me in Paradise."* As we studied above, Jesus made a promise to the criminal who accepted him minutes before his death. The criminal's faith had outgrown his sin; he humbly acknowledged the Savior and simply asked Jesus to remember him. And Jesus did. Jesus desires each of us to share eternity with him, so much so, that he will never give up on us.

4. *"Father, into your hands I commend my spirit."* Our Savior gave all glory to God throughout his ministry, and into the safety of His Almighty hands he placed himself as he left this world. To God these words signaled fulfillment of the promise He had made to mankind and the eminent reunion awaiting them in Heaven. To Satan these words would have been a dagger through the heart as he realized his failure to turn Jesus his way. Evil could not bribe, tempt, beat, persecute or drive a single wedge between Father and His only begotten Son. God calls us to such a bond where evil has no room to come between us.

5. *"Woman, behold your son."* and *"Behold your mother."* For Catholics especially, this proclamation has significant meaning as we honor the mother of Christ as the "Mother" of our holy and apostolic church, the universal body of Christ. Mary's role as mother was instituted through the annunciation when she agreed to the will of God to bear not just a son, but also a Savior. Jesus personalized God in a way not previously understood and then invited us to share in this intimacy by calling his Father, our Father ("Our

Father, who art in heaven.") From upon the cross, Jesus proclaimed our shared mother. In this important and timely exchange, Jesus gave his own mother to the disciple John. Jesus also gave the disciple John to his blessed mother. In honoring Mary as our mother we honor Christ. In turn, Our Blessed Mother honors her Son by watching over us.

6. *"I thirst."* What ALL was Jesus thirsting for? Did he thirst physically because of the demands placed upon his beaten and crucified body? Perhaps, for it is an instinctual need when a racked body intensely thirsts to replenish lost liquids. But, as we studied above, Jesus' thirst also had emotional and spiritual undertones. A thirst for the criminal's repentance foreshadowed Jesus' thirst for our repentance. Inviting Jesus into our desperate lives is like installing an everlasting well within us. When we satisfy the thirsting Jesus upon the cross we too will be forever satisfied.

7. *"It is finished."* Why did Jesus choose the word *"It"* to describe what was finished? Jesus did not say, "I am finished." These words cause us to consider how Jesus viewed his days on earth. It never was about him, *it* was about *his mission* to fulfill the will of his Father in Heaven. Will we be able to emulate Jesus in this way and to say at the end of our life, *"it* is finished?" What exactly does *it* mean within our lives? If we all are placed on earth for a particular purpose, should we not also consider our life as a checklist of God's will and our death as a completion or fulfillment of that list? So submissive was the Son of God that he chose to end his perfect life of ministry, teaching and passion in the same humble way it began. From the wood of a manger to the wood of the cross, Jesus remained faithful to God. *It* represents his purpose. *It* represents his life. *It* paid for our sins. *It* serves as our example. *It* ended so the resurrection could begin and so with his resurrection we may also be resurrected. By the way, in the book of Revelation 16:17, what words do you think come from the throne of God at the end of the Seven **Last** Plagues upon Earth? As the **last** angel poured out its contents upon the earth, the throne of God roars, *"it* is

done." From the beginning of time to the second coming of Jesus, *it* seems to be a recurring theme of progress toward the ultimate plan of God's will. Thanks be to God that *it* will conclude with us on His side!

DISCUSSION CORNER

Using the words of Christ from the cross and the points listed above, why do you think Jesus chose these phrases to emphasize? What do these words mean in your life? How do you interpret his messages of abandonment, forgiveness, submissiveness, thirst and humility? How do you answer his invitation to join him in paradise and to share with him in the love for and gifts from his own mother?

Read the seven statements again as if Jesus speaks them timelessly and personally to you.

As we have seen throughout his ministry and again in his final words, Jesus holds nothing back in aiding us through our journey. How can you better utilize these heartfelt gifts from the cross of your Savior?

HUNGRY SOULS NEED TO BE FED

A True Story . . .

Several years ago I visited Vatican City in Italy. I was so excited for this part of the trip and allowed my anticipation to set my expectations. I wanted to be moved, guided, educated and spiritually filled. I left feeling sad, disgusted, disappointed and spiritually emptied. Our tour guide was secularly disposed, speaking only of the value or history of the artwork and structures. His reverence seemed oddly rooted and absent of any spiritual perspective whatsoever . . . like describing a crucifix as a piece of forged metal shaped like a man atop two pieces of beautifully hand carved olive wood. This drove me crazy. So often I wanted to interrupt him because he was missing the point. "It's a crucifix, for heaven's sake! The man who inspired this work died for you. Did you forget that? It isn't about the wood. It's about the man on the wood."

The tour guide's pedantic views continued to erase my hopes for a spiritually filled afternoon, so I finally removed the wireless headset connection between us and began experiencing the holy ground on my own. My heart would not settle. I wanted to be spoon fed from its delicious bounty, to savor every detail, to chew on the antiquity and to gulp-down its essence. I was strolling beside one of the greatest spiritual banquet tables on Earth . . . with my hands tied behind my back! Frustrated, I left the holy city hoping never to return.

It was only recently I changed my mind. A Catholic talk radio station I listen to was broadcasting from their pilgrimage within Vatican City. The group was too large for one tour guide so they split into two.

It was amazing as the two groups described their experiences. One tour had a similar experience to mine while the other group went on and on about the way the guide truly "led" them through the halls, allowed them time to reflect at certain pieces, encouraged them and demonstrated spiritual reverence at some of the more profound selections.

The light bulb went on for me . . . not all guides are created equal. There are guides for the secular world (necessary for the many who come daily to study and view the art) and there are guides for the spiritual world (necessary to feed all our hungry souls).

The opportunity to return presented itself and so I booked another trip to Vatican City. I scoured the Internet for information on tours, questioned a few fellow travelers, read a bunch of reviews and then scrutinized the company before booking the tour. Then, upon meeting the guide outside the Vatican, I politely interrogated her again. Was it worth it? Well . . . It was an amazing experience and I was fed beyond my imagination from the bountiful banquet. If you ever have the chance to visit Vatican City, I hope you go. I also hope you learn from my experience so you too might be spiritually fulfilled.

ENTERING NOW, THE HOLY SPIRIT

"O Holy Spirit, descend plentifully into my heart. Enlighten the dark corners of this neglected dwelling and scatter there Thy cheerful beams." Saint Augustine

Because of the Holy Spirit, many can read the Bible without interpretation and gain necessary wisdom and knowledge. Some say it is as simple as praying for advice, randomly opening to a page and then reading until you yield fruitful insight. The Holy Spirit guides many new and veteran readers to deeper understandings. Theologians, priests and religious leaders labor to help us more deeply understand the timing, relevance, and complexity woven throughout the books of the Bible. They guide us to the truths and help us equate and apply ancient teachings to modern challenges.

We would not understand the intricacies of the Bible, nor would we even have a New Testament to contemplate, had it not been for others' tireless hours of work in translation, insight, and intuition. The early Church Fathers and saints received wisdom and direction in interpreting the Bible as a whole, linking important stories, traditions and prophesy of the Old to the New.

The *Catechism of the Catholic Church* is a beautiful compilation of many of those teachings, documenting the research and philosophies of theologians and saints who accurately interpreted the meaning of Holy Scripture. Below is one such entry regarding the importance of the Holy Spirit:

Catholic Link

Catechism of the Catholic Church

2681 "No one can say 'Jesus is Lord,' except by the Holy Spirit" (*1 Cor* 12:3). The Church invites us to invoke the Holy Spirit as the interior Teacher of Christian prayer.

The Roman Catholic Church teaches much of the Bible using visuals and repetition. It is no wonder this is the case, when you realize its roots. The

Bible came from the church, not the church from the Bible. Think about that, for it represents how far back the Catholic Church stretches. The completion of gathering New Testament books was not fully formalized by the church for nearly 400 years! Through the wisdom of the Holy Spirit, Pope St. Innocent I, in 405 A.D., approved the 73-book canon (27 NT and 46 OT books) and closed it from any further additions or changes. (note 6-1)

The Holy Spirit, who descended upon the apostles at Pentecost, led them to institute holy tradition. Jesus may not have left them with a playbook, but he did leave the Holy Spirit to coach and guide them. The Holy Spirit whispered encouragement, brought back vivid memories of their days with Jesus, aided in their writings and taught them how to spread the news of the Messiah.

The letters from Paul to the Romans, Corinthians, Galatians, etc., were happening in real-time as they were read aloud to congregations of new believers. Traditions were quickly set using Christ's own words and actions as the eternal template for liturgical services. Memorable pictures, the parables taught by Jesus and stories of healings were all tools used by the early church to present Christianity. This tradition was strengthened through repetition and allowed even disparate languages, customs and educational levels to all share in the same Word of God. Many of those original traditions shaped the Mass (Liturgy) celebrated within the early Church communities.

In fact, the Mass we celebrate today remains, at its core, the same celebration taught by the apostles to the first Christian communities. We know from recovered early writings such as the Didache (Teaching of the Apostles) and Saint Justin the Martyr that the general format and structure of our Liturgy (Mass) was already in place by the year 150. (note 6-2)

As history already proved throughout the Old Testament, whenever the Jewish people were lacking firm direction they began turning back to idol worship and other God-less pleasures. Tradition and repetition, guided by the Holy Spirit, would be important. Therefore, the early Christian communities both recognized and adopted one universal body and one set of rules.

In the early years after Christ's resurrection, tradition was needed to balance the widespread persecution of Christians. During this time, most of the historical documents speaking of Christianity were burned or buried. People found with Christian documents or Bibles were immediately killed, but the tradition forever engrained in their hearts and minds could not be destroyed. Had the Holy Spirit not instructed the Apostles to rely on and teach holy tradition through consistent repetition, the spread of Christianity might have died with the martyrs.

St. Paul writes to the church of Corinth, then to the church of the Thessalonians, on heeding sacred tradition:

> *Be imitators of me, as I am of Christ. I praise you because you remember me in everything and hold fast to the traditions, just as I handed them on to you. 1 Corinthians 11:1-2*

> *Therefore, brothers, stand firm and hold fast to the traditions that you were taught, either by an oral statement or by a letter of ours. 2 Thessalonians 2:15*

Once the dust of persecution settled near the end of the second century, the leaders of "The Church" began compiling books they believed to be canonical. It was not until the end of the fourth century, however, that the full translation into Latin supplied the first Bible.

It was not until 1529, when Martin Luther led a protest moving away from the Roman Catholic Church that seven books, a chapter and a few verses were dropped from the Old Testament, leaving what is known today as the Protestant Bible. All twenty-seven New Testament books, as were approved in 405 A.D., were retained within the Protestant Bible; however, not all of the original interpretation was retained. (Note 6-3)

Theologians have identified many reasons for and against dropping the Old Testament books, but Catholics should feel honored to own a copy of the original historical books. The same words read during the life of

Jesus are forever preserved and retained by the Roman Catholic Church, through the direction and wisdom of the Holy Spirit, for our use and contemplation.

SCRIPTURE + TRADITION = MASS

Have you ever been reading the Bible and found words quoted directly from the Mass written on its pages? You may have initially thought our Liturgy Service (Mass) was all tradition except for the Scripture readings and singing of the Psalms, but the words, structure, and components of our holy Mass are actually scattered throughout the pages of the Bible. In fact, you can't properly interpret one without knowing the other, because they are so tightly woven together. Likewise, the knowledge of each casts a light of understanding onto the other, helping us gain more insight into the words of Scripture and the symbols within the Mass.

The following verses should sound familiar if you attend Catholic Mass. Listen for them next Sunday and bask in the sacred tradition intentionally preserved for you.

Matthew 20: 30-34—is a glimpse of our introduction to Mass. *Lord, have mercy. Christ, have mercy. Lord, have mercy.* The blind men were asking for the Lord to have pity on them so they might be healed. This passage translates to our opening prayer at Mass. We also approach God's house as blind sinners, humbly seeking forgiveness first so our eyes may be opened to God's Word. Jesus' example of stopping everything to answer the penitent hearts of the blind men resonates through the apostles, who followed his footsteps for compassion and healing. Time after time throughout the New Testament God granted miracles through the apostles and showed pity to those who earnestly sought mercy. No wonder we begin each Mass in this manner. By reciting the prayer at the instruction and prompting of the priest: *Lord, have mercy, Christ, have mercy, Lord, have mercy,* we invoke a request for clemency from the Highest Power. How sweet is the reward of a humbled heart! So if ever you run a tad bit late for Mass you may want to consider the prayer you missed and ask for your own share of that mercy before you walk in.

Mark 11: 9-10—Just before we kneel for the consecration of the Eucharist, we all recite a prayer of entrance and adoration. *Holy, Holy, Holy Lord God of hosts. Heaven and earth are full of your glory. Hosanna in the highest. Blessed is he who comes in the name of the Lord. Hosanna in the highest.* On the day we now call Palm Sunday, the crowds in Jerusalem uttered this prayer upon Jesus' arrival into the city. Jesus was announced and welcomed by this crowd just as we proclaim him before he comes into our presence through the Eucharist. That prayer ushered in the week of sacrifice for Jesus and the week of salvation for us. Jesus responded to the prayer then as he continues to do for us today . . . with compassion and longing for each of us.

1 Corinthians 11: 23-26—relates directly to the words the priest says during the consecration when the bread and wine are sanctified into the body and blood of Christ through transubstantiation. Notice that Paul states in verse 23 this "tradition" came from the Lord Jesus and was now being shared with them.

Luke 7: 6-10—where our pre-communion prayer comes from. *Lord, I am not worthy that you should enter under my roof, but only say the word and my soul shall be healed.* Jesus was so moved by the man's faith in this passage because the man recognized the divine authority of Jesus to command miracles—even from a distance. The owner of the slave, although wealthy and affluent, claimed he was not worthy for Jesus to enter his household (under his roof). He wished not to trouble the Lord further en route to his house yet trusted that if Jesus merely spoke it to be so, his slave could be healed. In preparation for receiving the Eucharist we too are first humbling ourselves, as did the owner of the slave, and then asking Jesus to speak the soul-cleansing word of healing. At each Mass, he answers the faithful prayer of his church for purification. From afar, and at the command of our Lord, our souls are healed. Then we, like the slave and his master with amazing faith, receive the miracle.

Revelation 16:17—should sound familiar as it honors the judgments of God similar to how we do in our prayer of response to the priest, who says, *"Let us give thanks to the Lord our God,"* and we say, *"It is right and just."*

Revelation 1:12-13—This represents the lampstands used to adorn the holy altars in our churches and the vestments worn by our priests. Several of the visions of John found in the book of Revelation were used to create the structure of our Mass, as these things were pleasing to God. The Catholic Church recreates, the best it can, what God has revealed to us from Heaven. John's vision fell heavily upon the early fathers of the Church as they discerned its meaning and symbolism. Our churches represent holy replicas of the throne of God in Heaven, using glimpses of His Almighty Kingdom to perfect our temples of adoration. Our reverence and attention to His Almighty detail, contained within John's vision, will be honored with His desire to dwell among us, to be Our God and for us to be His people.

Revelation 8:3-4—Be careful, this visual may make you wish we had incense at every Mass! Wow, just picture the angel of God standing beside our altars of worship, raising our prayers with the smoke of the incense and creating for our prayers a fine and fragrant wrapping of sorts. He calls us His holy ones and He does hear our prayers. Wafting high above the altar are the angels who came to gather the prayers of the faithful during our Mass and to take them to the very throne of God.

By now, you probably get the idea that Holy Scripture is linked to the Catholic Mass, although many more correlations still exist scattered through the pages of the Bible. The point of this exercise is two-fold.

First, it is to bring more of the Mass to life through placing its words back into scriptural context. We don't just say words to be saying words. Each part of the Mass has a sacred purpose, is pleasing to God, and is a preserved version of what was taught to the first Christian believers.

Second, it is to illustrate that removing Scripture from our Mass would be like unraveling yarn from a sweater. Scripture alone is like a skein of yarn, open for the interpretation of the knitter. The Mass' traditions weave scripture into the sweater, the blanket, and the socks so we can see its fulfillment come to life for purpose and common use. The more we go to Mass, the larger our wardrobe of wisdom becomes. The larger the wardrobe, the better we can protect ourselves in all seasons of life. The traditions of the Catholic Church are carefully built upon the actions and words of Christ, creating for all generations a timeless treasure.

Clothe yourself with the radiant hand-me-downs of the apostles. (Spoken by Jesus to the apostles after his resurrection but before the Holy Spirit descended upon them. The Holy Spirit clothed the apostles, and those clothes are still being "handed down" to us through the holy church!)

> *Then he opened their minds to understand the scriptures. And [behold] I am sending the promise of my Father upon you; but stay in the city until you are clothed with power from on high."*
> Luke 24:45,49

THE CRUCIFIX

> *'Take the holy crucifix in your hands, kiss its wounds with great love, and ask Him to preach you a sermon. Listen to what the thorns, the nails, and that Divine Blood say to you. Oh! What a sermon." (St. Paul of the Cross)*

As for many of us, we would not know Jesus the way we know Jesus, if not for the Crucifix. It provokes us to wonder and engages us in the story of his life. A stable and manger scene portrays the humble birth of baby Jesus while the crucifix portrays his humble death.

Catholic tradition is credited with remembering Jesus upon the cross and keeping alive the true story of love and sacrifice through the crucifix. Jesus embraced the sin-laden cross for us and then died upon it, redeeming the sins of mankind. It was not the wood of the cross that saved us; it was Christ upon the cross that saved us. Alone, the cross stirs many spiritual and emotional feelings, yet it is the crucifix that immediately humbles us, calling us to a deeper and more reverent respect. It reminds us of a call to sacrifice—both Christ's and our own—while supplying us with the Almighty measuring stick (wooden of course), on which we are asked to continuously grow.

Far too many Christian religions forego the use of crucifixes in their churches. How many generations will it take before they forget the meaning of the cross? How vividly can we teach the story when the visual is missing? Will a generation of barren crosses grow barren hearts to sacrifice?

God has been removed from public schools and we have witnessed the gradual deterioration of our young people's values. For example, it is interesting to ponder how the exact same "book" is regulated differently in two United States government institutions. While one institution has forbidden its use the other proclaims its worth and widely uses it for direction and correction. The government institutions are public schools and penitentiaries. The book, of course, is the Bible. Why do we withhold this valuable treasure and resource from our children when we know the power it contains?

It is easy to forget what is not there. There is no worthy substitute for God in our schools and there is no worthy substitute for Jesus upon the cross. Both will teach simply by their presence. If we remove the teacher from the student how can we hold the student accountable?

> "In that one and the same event, there is the sign of sin's utter depravity and the seal of divine forgiveness. From that point on, no man can look upon a crucifix and say that sin is not serious, nor can he ever say that it cannot be forgiven. By the way He suffered, He revealed the reality of sin; by the way He bore it, He shows His mercy toward the sinner." (Archbishop Fulton Sheen)

DISCUSSION CORNER

As we look upon the crucifix, we see that Jesus chose to accept the route of pain and suffering to pay for our salvation. In return, what pain (or perhaps just discomfort) can we stop avoiding for him? What can we steer ourselves into, instead of away from, for the glory of God? For each of us this cross looks different yet it is what we are all called to do as we follow him.

It may entail forgiving, protecting, noticing, remembering, or ministering to someone. Perhaps you are being nudged to give up something or accept a new challenge. It could be something as small as sending a card to someone, as big as a total change in direction for your life, or anything in between. You may even want to ask the others in your group for some guidance. Often times it is others who first articulate or confirm for us our unique set of God-given skills, which we simply take for granted. Piecing together what others perceive as value within us can lead to our own awakening.

Whatever we are called to do today, tomorrow or in the future, remember that it will most certainly fall outside of our cozy and warm comfort zone. If it did not, it would not be a sacrifice. Our only guarantees when picking up a cross is that Jesus will be in front to lead us, the Holy Spirit will be there to strengthen us and God will keep our journey within the boundary of His grace.

THE SIGN OF THE CROSS

*Then I looked and there was the Lamb standing on Mount Zion,
and with him a hundred and forty-four thousand who had his name
and his Father's name written on their foreheads. Revelations 14:1*

We begin a prayer with . . . the sign of the cross. We open our Mass with . . . the sign of the cross. We end each blessing with . . . the sign of the cross. Before we enter into troubled waters we beckon . . . the sign of the cross. And after a victory (or even a touchdown) we kneel to give thanks with . . . the sign of the cross.

The sign of the cross has become an international language of blessing and thanksgiving. It is one of the most basic prayers of the Catholic Church (yes, it is a prayer in and of itself) and there is no mistaking its identity and its reference to the Holy Trinity—of Father, Son, and Holy Spirit. Its inference stands alone.

Catholic Link

Catechism of the Catholic Church

2157 The Christian begins his day, his prayers, and his activities with the Sign of the Cross: "in the name of the Father and of the Son and of the Holy Spirit. Amen." The baptized person dedicates the day to the glory of God and calls on the Savior's grace which lets him act in the Spirit as a child of the Father. The sign of the cross strengthens us in temptations and difficulties.

This outward sign of making the "Sign of the Cross" is first introduced to the Christian during baptism. The priest, parents and godparents make this sign on our foreheads.

A slight variation to the sign of the cross comes during our Mass, just before reading the gospel, when the priest invites us to join him in making three crosses—on our forehead, over our lips, and over our heart. The significance of the little crosses at this particular time in the Mass is intriguing. Because Scripture is so important to the Liturgy, we are asked to take a moment to pray for insight and wisdom as the words are being read to us. We are to pray for the Word of God to be ever present in our minds (as we touch our forehead), as we speak (as we touch our lips), and in our hearts (as we cross our hearts.)

We, who bless ourselves with the sign of the cross throughout our lives, do not do it to show others *who* we are, but rather *whose* we are.

LET US PRAY

Oh crucified Christ and perfect Lamb of God, let it be that we never know a day that we do not thank you for your sacrifice. Instill in us a humility that will keep us close to you, grounded in faith and rooted in love. Send your Holy Spirit to fill the hearts of your faithful followers and open our eyes to the power of your holy Eucharist.

Thank you for the saints who blazed trails ahead of us by their obedience to the will of God. Help us to follow their example. Help us to gain your heavenly peace so we might leave the imprint of our Creator upon the world. Not our will, but your Almighty will through us, be done.

Sixth Prayer: The Crucifixion

The prayer of St. Bridget for the Crucifixion

Pray 1 Our Father, 1 Hail Mary, then:

Eternal Father, through Mary's unblemished hands and the Divine Heart of Jesus, I offer You Your Son on the Cross, His Nailing and Raising, His Wounds on the Hands and Feet and the three streams of His Precious Blood that poured forth from these for us, His extreme tortures of the Body and Soul, His precious Death and its non-bleeding Renewal in all Holy Masses on earth as atonement for all wounds against vows and regulations within the Orders, as reparation for my and all of the world's sins, for the sick and the dying, for all holy priests and laymen, for the Holy Father's intentions toward the restoration of Christian families, for the strengthening of Faith, for our country and unity among all nations in Christ and His Church, as well as for the Diaspora.

The Piercing of Jesus' Side

Bible passages needed for study of this chapter:

John 19:31-37	Zechariah 12:10	Ephesians 6:10-17
Luke 23:47	John 20:24-29	

Please read John 19:31-37.

This was the last time Jesus would shed blood for us. He entirely emptied himself before leaving this world, holding back nothing to save the ones he loved.

You just read the only gospel to include the shedding of blood and water from the pierced side of Jesus. The gospels of Matthew, Mark and Luke move from death of Christ to his burial but the author of John adds, and testifies to the truth of, this momentary yet monumental occurrence. Remember how Luke's gospel was the only one to give us the droplets of blood mixed with sweat in the Agony of the Garden chapter? Likewise, John's addition is purposeful as it links Old Testament prophesies to Jesus. The authors of the gospels sought not only to corroborate the most popular stories of Jesus but to also enlighten certain truths beyond them. However the author came to add this particular chronicle to the narrative story of Jesus, he must also have felt the need to defend it (verse 35).

Perhaps this truth from the cross was safely contained within an intimate and loyal group at first, and then deliberately revealed when the time was appropriate. As the popularity of Christianity grew so did the stories about Jesus. Early Christians were tasked with carefully validating the circulating stories or miracles of the Messiah since a mixture of truths, half-truths, fabrications and gossip would now spread like wildfire across their communities.

When you think about it, validation could be difficult considering the way Jesus operated. Many times he would work privately as he addressed the yearning souls of the faithful, healing people in ways the apostles would not have understood at the time. These stories would be like seedlings whose growth would mature after word spread of Jesus' death and resurrection.

The corroborated miracle healings and stories about him would lend credence to the now established Savior's story, and surely the apostles were grateful for them. Word of mouth helped Christianity rapidly blossom but also would have been used by disbelievers as a conduit to circulate stories of doubt and deception. Some initial evidence, like the piercing in the side of Jesus, may have seemed unimportant yet grew in significance over time as more truths about this moment were discovered. In fact, the piercing in the side of Jesus must have been a particularly strong or controversial revelation, as the gospel itself states that it was included, ". . . *that you also may come to believe*".

Old Testament Holy Scripture is sighted within this passage; referring to the condition of his bones and the piercing his body would endure. We will link these passages later but now it is time to learn a little more about the man on the other end of the lance.

THE SOLDIER STANDING WATCH

His name was Longinus and he probably woke up that morning thinking it was going to be just another day at the office. He was wrong. Upon reporting to duty he probably heard the rumbling over the man named Jesus and the conviction he was now ordered to carry out. We do not know where he stood in relationship to Christ prior to this day but we have to believe, by his actions, this was a routine crucifixion for him. *Bad guys have to pay their debts.* His job was to make sure justice was served and he was good at his job. He was a Roman soldier and a puissant knight (note 7-1), well trained in military combat and warfare. He still wore a wound from one such conflict which should have affected his ability to serve, but being assigned to Jesus this day validates he was a powerful and respected soldier.

As the story goes, Longinus had been injured during battle. This injury left him nearly blind. Still the soldier used his intact resources to defend his turf upon Calvary by keeping bystanders away from the criminals' bodies and making sure those bodies remained attached to their crosses . . . until, that is, they had permission to release the dead bodies. After the bodies were taken down his job would be completed for the day. He could go home to rest until his barbarous skills were once again needed to defend the ancient Roman Empire.

This particular crucifixion day posed a bit of a wrinkle to normal operating procedure, however, as the Sabbath of this week coincided with a major Jewish Holy day. Only three times a year did the Jewish people travel to celebrate feasts and this was one of them.

Having eaten the Passover meal the night before, this crucifixion day would begin their holy and sacred Feast of Unleavened Bread. People were eager to get home for holiday and Sabbath preparations and therefore requested the crucifixion be "hurried up" a bit so they could go on about their solemn holiday. As ironic as it seems now it probably made all the sense in the world to the soldiers standing watch; if they should hasten the kill of Jesus, there would be more time to pray to God.

As instructed, the soldiers were to break the legs of the criminals so they could no longer lift themselves to gain a breath. Criminals hanging on crosses used their leg muscles as long as they could, mustering needed strength to clear the passageway for air to move in and out of their lungs. The more tired their bodies became, the less they could be lifted to achieve the necessary position to intake and exhale air. Eventually the breaths of the crucified would become shallow and infrequent. Soon after, they would die of suffocation.

Breaking the legs insured a speedy death for two of the three on crosses that holy day outside of Jerusalem. The one named Jesus, hanging in the middle of the other two, was already dead when the centurion approached. Just to make sure Longinus decided to thrust his own spear into the side of Jesus. As he did so both water and blood poured forth from the side of Jesus. Upon the soldier and onto his spear fell droplets of our Lord's precious blood, which immediately healed the sight of the centurion.

What blindness had kept hidden in the shadows, sight now revealed. Longinus had just participated in the death of not only a righteous man but, moreover, his Savior. Please read the words attributed to Longinus found within Luke 23:47, for his life would never be the same after the sacred blood of the Lamb touched him.

SAINT LONGINUS AND THE INAUGURAL MIRACLE

According to the legend of Saint Longinus (note 7-2), he gained more than his eyesight that day. For not only his eyes, but also his heart, were opened for the Savior. With this new and everlasting vision, he dedicated himself to the work of spreading the Good News of Jesus Christ.

It all started when Jesus, the man Longinus had just tortured into excruciating death, decided to single him out to receive an amazing miracle! Not just any miracle but an inaugural blessing of sorts. Jesus was dead (verified by the spear) yet his miracles did not stop with his death.

Therefore, this would have been Jesus' first recorded miracle after humanity had been emptied from his body. This is yet another indication that God does not tire of us and like Father like Son, they didn't even take a break.

Moments after his death, while still hanging from the cross, Jesus reached out to help mankind through a miracle handmade for the heart of Longinus. How did God work to prepare this heart to accept the gift that would soon rain down upon him, knowing that his acceptance of this gift would be used to proclaim God's endless glory?

Perhaps Longinus had wondered about Jesus before this day and maybe even heard him speak once or twice. Or maybe he was aware of the miracles attributed to him and had secretly hoped to meet him, knowing he could sure use a miracle. The conviction of Jesus would have caused any good thoughts to disappear, however, as the judgment fell against the man who was now considered to be a fake. Longinus would not have questioned the ruling, as he was paid well to keep and follow the orders of the Roman Empire. There is also the chance that Longinus' only knowledge of Jesus came from the day he crucified him. In that case, Jesus would have softened his heart from the cross, through his words and example.

At some point after the miracle took place, Longinus found and then began to follow the apostles. Legend says he was baptized into Christianity, abandoned his former life and became a monk. He drove evil from towns in the name of Christ, setting free those who listened and believed. For thirty-eight years he lived to tell his story among the people of Caesarea and Cappadocia and many were converted because of his faith, including the officer who eventually martyred him.

A full circle of events began with Jesus. Longinus put Jesus to death and consequently was saved by him; Longinus' last prayer saved the provost who put him to death. The incredible story goes something like this. After the chief officer had brought charges against Longinus for refusing to worship idols he had him condemned to death. (It is reported that nothing short of death could stop Longinus from worshiping God and converting men, as he had already had his mouth cut open and teeth removed, yet he could still preach his message with clarity to all who would listen.) One brave man stood up for Longinus and, because of it, had his tongue removed by the provost in charge. (This must have been a popular practice!) Immediately upon laying a hand on the one who defended Longinus, blindness and severe pain struck the provost.

Longinus saw his opportunity to convert one last soul before his impending death and told the provost he would pray to God that, in exchange for his own death, God might restore the provost's health. The provost, who was now writhing in pain, without haste martyred Longinus by beheading him; all the while hoping that Longinus' last prayer to God might indeed be answered with a miracle to relieve his pain. The provost, after killing Longinus, immediately fell upon his body and begged for forgiveness. God did indeed grant the forgiveness and, through the intercession of Longinus, the miracles continued as all health was once again restored to the provost. It was now the provost who would carry the torch of Christianity forward.

The crucifixion of Jesus stirred many people's hearts that day. Some hearts were further hardened and some, like Longinus, were ripe for his compassion. Some people viewed him as a Savior and others, a criminal. Some were pre-occupied with the holy and sacred festivities at hand—in other words, more worried about the holiday "lamb for God" to be roasted than the "Lamb of God" hanging lifeless on the cross.

A DILEMMA OF SORTS

A True Story . . .

My husband and I were planning our first major event after the birth of our first daughter. It was for her baptism day and all of the family (both sides) would be coming back to our house for dinner afterwards. As a fairly competent cook, I decided to create a menu that would highlight my culinary skills, thereby impressing my family and family-in-laws.

I do not remember what the spectacular dish was but the timing of the whole process was giving me fits. Everything needed to be placed in the oven, stirred or set out right about the time the waters of baptism would be running over the head of my little infant girl. Still I panicked and then actually thought for a moment I had come up with the perfect solution. I could either leave the baptism a bit early or perhaps miss it all together so everything at home would be just perfect when our families arrived.

That is when **I** realized **I** had a problem! (Self-diagnosed)

How could I even think of slipping out of the baptism—or not even going—when that was truly the single most important part of the day? I was appalled at my own audacity to even plot such a thing. Begging for forgiveness, I reworked it somehow—allowing the baptism back up on center stage.

I'd like to say I learned my lesson but I still struggle during the Christian holidays, trying to catch myself before allowing God's feast and my feast to battle it out. When the winner is my feast, it is always a disappointment. When the winner is God's, I am always fulfilled.

DISCUSSION CORNER

Think about your Christmas and Easter holidays. How would you rank your current priorities and have they changed over time? Are your personal priorities reflected in the actions of those you spend the holidays with? How do you normally "feel" at the end of a sacred holiday? Are you blessed like our brother Longinus or frustrated like so many others who gathered around the cross that day?

Share your strategy of keeping God illuminated and on center stage when the world continues to limelight other enticing, albeit empty, promises.

Discuss your thoughts and hold yourself accountable to strengthen the weak or vulnerable areas blocking you from obtaining an even holier and more fulfilling life.

End by praying for the intercession of St. Longinus to share with us his zeal for Jesus and steadfast faith. Ask him to pray for us that we might emulate his courage and compassion for spreading the love of Jesus Christ, our Savior.

OLD TESTAMENT PROPHESIES

The gospel of John 19:31-37 that we read above records the fulfillment of two Old Testament prophesies in verses 36 and 37. Let's review them now and then trace them backwards. One says the Messiah would not incur any broken bones while the other states he will be pierced. Where did those words appear in Holy Scripture and why?

The verse of Psalms 34:21 contains the first clue about the bones of Jesus.

> *He watches over all his bones;*
> *not one of them shall be broken.*

The Psalms were praises to God known also as the "music of Israel," created, written, and compiled by various people over hundreds of years. These verses were sung or prayed in their temples for worship. We often think of King David when we think of the psalms, and rightfully so, as he loved music and inspired many of the verses. Seventy-three of the 150 psalms are attributed to him, yet his exact connection is unknown. Since King David was a chosen servant of God and the leader of God's holy people, it is easy to understand that his plight would become their plight; his joy, their joy, etc. Therefore many psalms would be credited to King David, possibly more as a communal passion than one of his alone.

The thirty-fourth Psalm shouts praises to God who has promised to deliver His people. It also is a psalm of thanksgiving for the refuge he has allowed them and the many blessings He has given to them. The verses are filled with wisdom, how to fear God and shun evil. Then comes verse 21, hidden among the verses of healing and wisdom, a verse about bones. Why bones, you might ask? Well, bones were considered sacred to ancient civilizations and it would not have seemed out of place at the time.

Broken bones were debilitating and caused prolonged weakness to the physical body. Unbroken bones signified strength of the person while living, and a person's bones would be the only part of a deceased body to remain after decay. God-fearing people buried their dead, respectfully preserving their sacred bones. Therefore, this verse would have meant more to them than it does to us with our advanced medical procedures and various burial methods.

Although the book of Psalms is not regarded as a prophetic book (meaning its contents were not of a prophet who spoke of the promised Messiah), it does contain clues about how God chose to announce and validate His son upon the Earth. The words contained in this specific verse about bones are illuminated with our knowledge of how the Messiah's bones were spared during his crucifixion. And although the people would not have specifically been looking for a Messiah with all his bones intact, the story would later reveal the hidden and mysterious prophesies of God's perfect plan!

Another such "non-prophetic" book is Exodus, where God is the one who instructs His people to follow a specific custom and then uses that pattern to reveal His son to the world. Chapter 12 of Exodus prescribes the annually recurring Passover ritual and verse 46 refers to the specifications for preparing and consuming the Passover lamb.

> It must be eaten in one house; you may not take any of its meat outside the house. You shall not break any of its bones.

God specifies earlier in the chapter (verse 5) that the lamb must be *without blemish* and its *blood* (verse 13) must be used to *mark the houses* from destruction. If you need a quick refresher as to the Passover feast so you can identify better with its correlation to Jesus' sacrifice for us, please take the time to read chapter 12 in its entirety. You will not be disappointed.

God's *unblemished* Son would die upon the cross shedding every ounce of his *blood* to *spare* all of mankind. Not one of his bones would be broken—as was foreshadowed by God himself to Moses and Aaron about 1500 years before he sent "His Lamb" to save us. Do you wonder if God might have winked or smiled a bit as he dictated the highly specific and somewhat peculiar ritual customs to the men of Israel, knowing he had only given them half the story?

Before we close our research on the bones of Jesus let's take a moment to reflect on their significance. The sins of mankind are very heavy and burdensome. One man made it his mission to gather them upon a cross and carry them for us. He struggled underneath their weight but he did not break. He hauled every single mortal and venial sin to the safety and finality of the cross where they died along with him.

As we well know, the heaviness of our own sin can break us still and more than our bones are subject to being shattered. Following our Savior is the only way to the truth and the light. Allow his love to sink into your bones, for in Him and through Him we will find strength.

Moving on to the piercing of Jesus, please open the prophetic book of Zechariah. Although other Scripture verses prophesize the piercing Jesus would endure, this one speaks specifically about the thrusting of our Savior. It is also rich in its prediction, written about 520 years before Christ. Let us end this prophesy section by reading the wisdom of Zechariah 12:10 and then looking to the Catechism of the Catholic Church for the correlation between his piercing and the conversion of our hardened hearts:

Catholic Link

Catechism of the Catholic Church

1432 The human heart is heavy and hardened. God must give man a new heart. [25] Conversion is first of all a work of the grace of God who makes our hearts return to him: "Restore us to thyself, O LORD, that we may be restored!" [26] God gives us the strength to begin anew. It is in discovering the greatness of God's love that our heart is shaken by the horror and weight of sin and begins to fear offending God by sin and being separated from him. The human heart is converted by looking upon him whom our sins have pierced: [27]

Let us fix our eyes on Christ's blood and understand how precious it is to his Father, for, poured out for our salvation, it has brought to the whole world the grace of repentance. [28]

[25] Cf. *Ezek* 36:26-27. [26] *Lam* 5:21. [27] Cf. *Jn* 19:37; *Zech* 12:10. [28] St. Clement of Rome, *Ad Cor.* 7, 4: PG 1, 224.

OUR SCARS DEFINE US

Warning: Meditating on these blood-shedding times of Jesus may cause you to rethink beauty. Some would have you believe that God looks past our wounds, wrinkles and scars to find our perfect beauty, but it is wrong to think in shallow human terms when trying to understand God. If we use Jesus as our model we will realize God looks upon our imperfections as beauty, especially when they mark a battle we fought for Him. From now on we should wear our outer markings of faith with pride, knowing whose "kingdom" they served.

Battles inevitably leave us wounded. Wounds heal over time but often leave scars. These marks may register in our human mind as imperfections, but God reveres them for their perfection in honoring Him. God raised Jesus from the dead on the third day. He had healed his wounds, cuts, and bruises. Jesus' heavenly body no longer felt physical pain yet God chose to leave behind the scars—through his side, on his hands, and on both of his feet. Why did God not restore His son's body to "unblemished beauty," clearing all scars brought on by man?

To his apostles, Jesus urged:

> *Look at my hands and my feet, that it is I myself. Touch me and see, because a ghost does not have flesh and bones as you can see I have." And as he said this, he showed them his hands and his feet. While they were still incredulous for joy and were amazed, he asked them, "Have you anything here to eat?" Luke 24:39-41*

And then to the still "doubting Thomas," who said he needed proof to believe, Jesus answered him also. Please open to John 20:24-29 to refresh your memory of the sincere doubt in Thomas' words and the specific markings that he required to see and touch so he might too believe Jesus had risen from the dead.

Jesus was able to give him proof because the scars of his crucifixion remained etched into his heavenly body. The scars of his loyal and willing death upon the cross of redemption defined who Jesus was to the apostles and still define him to us today through Holy Scripture. God left them so we would know His love. He left them so we would recognize our Savior. God revered the beauty in the wounds that saved us and glorified them to the apostles who sought desperately to believe.

Likewise, our scars will define us to God. They will follow us into heaven. What scars will you bring as gifts to your Creator? What challenges have you found on Earth worthy of a battle and for what crusade will you be remembered? What mark did you leave on the world that inevitably left its mark on you?

There are people who have given up everything to follow a call of God's will. They amaze us with their soothing disposition. Some walk away from wealth, success and prominence to fill a need while others use their gifts to help important causes in extraordinary ways. Many struggle with the call at first but never look back after accepting the challenge and the inherent wounds that come with the job.

God sets us up with earthly strengths that we might use them for Him. We are quick to stockpile the blessings but when called to the field we often are shocked. *Who, me?*

Satan loves luring the chosen in; first allowing God to spend years training, polishing, promoting, and equipping his guard, then waiting for us to receive our marching orders. That is when Satan lies to us. He might even tell us that we have become *too important* to listen to God. Perhaps we are *too busy* or *too scared* to venture beyond our zone of comfort. Many times we just think we are *not ready* for what He is calling us to do. It is okay to doubt but we must remain faithful to the gifts we accepted that brought us to this point. Like Jesus was saying to his Father in the garden of Gethsemane, we should also be . . .

> *saying, "Father, if you are willing, take this cup away from me; still, not my will but yours be done." Luke 22:42*

We would all be sunk if Jesus had changed his mind and chose to follow his own agenda. Human agendas are weak and vulnerable; divine agendas are what we are programmed for. God abundantly blessed His only begotten

Son: Jesus could perform endless miracles, he spoke with great wisdom and his teachings made him popular, trusted, and loved among his many followers. But the last supper arrived and it was time to settle up for the sins of mankind, and even he wondered if he was ready.

God calls us to action when He knows we are ready for the battle even when we might doubt our readiness. Our faith is often the only weapon we think we have when we step from our security into the dangerous arena of war. God has qualified us and now he needs us, so we are asked to go.

Since it was not the will of God to take the cup away from Jesus, he stood up from his prayer in the Garden of Gethsemane and walked straight into the battle awaiting him. God allowed evil to unleash its fury upon the sinless man, so all sinners could be reconciled through His Son's suffering and sacrifice.

And then—Our God began to count. He and the angels surrounding Jesus numbered the wounds, the stripes, the punctures, the nail holes, and every single infraction to the body and tender heart of Jesus. Not one blow went unnoticed and not one sigh was overlooked. God used every sacrifice, every fast and every prayer offering for His great glory and the atonement for our sins. God's beloved Son died at the hand of evil, but rose in victory for his Father and for each of us.

God still uses our sacrifices, our fasting, and our prayer offerings for atonement and reconciliation. Not a single one of our sacrifices is uncounted by God, as we strive to follow the example of Jesus. We can change the world through prayer because prayer is where God meets us, strengthens us and protects us.

Please open your Bible to Ephesians 6:10-17 and study the words of Paul.

He teaches us about true strength and how to "put on" the armor of God. Notice the last verse and its relevance to studying Holy Scripture. No wonder Mother Teresa had the following quote:

"When I was crossing into the Gaza, I was asked at the checkpost whether I was carrying any weapons. I replied: Oh yes, my prayer books." Mother Teresa

Allow yourself to wonder what God could do with us if we viewed scars differently. What if we courageously faced the will of God and followed Him, no matter where he took us? We have the perfect example of what pleased God, so if we truly want to be like Christ, then we too will leave this world a bit battered and bruised, cut and scraped. The wounds will heal, but God does not forget a single suffering that brought Him glory. Our scars will tell the story of our lives on earth and will mark the causes we knew we had to fight for.

DISCUSSION CORNER

Many lifestyles viewed on Earth as successful fail miserably when it comes to the litmus test in heaven. What types of successes impress you? Be honest about the lure of both good and evil. We all must possess both or else we would never sin. Does the carefree lifestyle of a rock star entice you or perhaps the glamour of a model or starlet? Perhaps you desire power over people, the ability to make millions or to discover the next medical cure or technological phenomenon.

The same thing that first seduces us could be the place God needs us to go. How else would he get us to move? It is only when we abandon His will for our own that we get into trouble. Talk about the dangers of the lifestyle you seek but also talk about the value and exposure of the same lifestyle placed in God's hands.

THE WATER

At the beginning of this chapter, we read from John's gospel about the piercing, which caused both blood and water to flow from the side of Jesus. We have studied several chapters on the blood-shedding times of Jesus, but will now conclude this book with the water.

When you think of the significance of water in relation to the church, you might think of its cleansing power such as is in the waters of baptism. You might also recall that it is water that cleanses the hands of the priest during Mass, washing away any iniquities before his hands become the mechanism for consecrating the unleavened bread into the body and blood of Christ. Holy water fonts greet us at the doors of our churches to offer us another layer of protection as we bless ourselves with the sign of the cross. And Holy Water comes raining down upon us during special occasion Masses when the priest walks the aisles of the church with the holy water vessel in hand.

If you are one who likes history, you may find it interesting to note the background of holy water within the church. Some ancient documents attribute the use of holy water as a tradition dating back to the apostle St. Matthew. (note 7-3) It is unclear how many of the apostles followed this tradition and why it was first proposed, but generations continue to discover buried documents that provide glimpses of the strong early church foundation used to build and proliferate the timeless traditions of Christianity. Holy Water was one of those sacred and useful traditions.

St. Faustina (1905-1938) gave us the image of the Divine Mercy of Jesus, in which Jesus is standing in a white robe while one hand is touching his heart. From his heart flow two sets of rays. One set is pale white and the other is red. In the book *Diary of St. Maria Faustina Kowalska*, St. Faustina records that Jesus revealed this picture to her. (note 7-4) He told her it represented the piercing in his side as endured at the end of his crucifixion.

From the very moment his precious blood and water spilled forth, Jesus asks us to take refuge within its everlasting hope. The sinfulness of mankind is to look upon these rays as a shelter for calling upon the generous gifts of mercy, which Jesus keeps contained within the rays of blood and water. The pale white ray signifies the water which makes souls righteous. Water is also a biblical sign of the Holy Spirit, the advocate given to us by Jesus. The red ray signifies the blood which is the life of our souls, brought to everlasting life through acceptance of the blood of our Savior.

Jesus set up his holy church on Earth to receive such mercy through the Sacraments of Baptism, Penance, and the Eucharist. The waters of Baptism initially cleanse our souls, while the Sacrament of Penance continues to keep it purified. The Sacrament of the Eucharist is indeed the body and blood of Christ used to continually nourish and strengthen our souls. These sacraments are tangible signs of his enduring mercy and love.

Jesus claimed to St. Faustina the magnitude of his great mercy—we are to trust in its bottomless depth! Try to imagine a "bottomless depth" of mercy and the meaning it holds for each one of us.

- ✓ There is no such thing as a sin too vast for the depths of the love of Christ Jesus.
- ✓ We do not have the ability to make unworthy what Jesus has already made worthy.
- ✓ Humans are incapable of exceeding the cost that was already paid in full.
- ✓ There is no sin that exists outside the realm of forgiveness, for forgiveness has no stopping point for Jesus.

Why then, do we choose to hold anything back from him? Why do we not trust in his mercy more? We knew this about his great love already, but St. Faustina causes us to attach a "bottomless" visual to an extraordinary kind of love. Earthly love needs to be guarded because it lives in a world of evil. Our capacity to love is limited by our own humanity. Heaven has no boundaries such as these, and the love Jesus offers to us is a "divine love." To know that kind of love, well . . . we just have to experience it.

The Catholic Church celebrates the feast of the Divine Mercy on the first Sunday following Easter and it is customary for the Image of Mercy, as first seen by St. Faustina, to be displayed. Jesus asked for this picture to serve as a refuge to many in need of his mercy for salvation. Many graces and abundant mercies are shown to the people who look upon this image on this day of holiness. Likewise, many graces continuously pour forth upon those who meditate upon the Passion of our Lord.

From the side of our Lord flowed blood and water, both of which we need for our sustenance on Earth. So whenever you remember the blood of our Lord, sacrificed on the altar of the cross for our salvation, remember too the water. Remember it when you reach your fingers into the Holy Water font at church, when you see the waters of Baptism flow over the baby who was just consecrated to God, and when you see the priest pour the water into the wine before consecration. Remember the significance and call upon its blessing. In it, you will find the mercy you seek.

Jesus taught the following prayer to St. Faustina. He desired her to pray it with a contrite heart for the sinners in need of conversion. Jesus told her that he desired their salvation even though they believed themselves unworthy. Oh, what a merciful Savior we have been sent by the God who loves us. The words, "Jesus, I trust in you" were also placed at the bottom of the painting which depicted the vision of Jesus by St. Faustina.

> *"O Blood and Water, which gushed forth from the Heart of Jesus as a fount of Mercy for us, I trust in You."* (Note 7-5)

THE BEGINNING

We pray:

Allow this ending to truly be a new beginning for us, as we continue to call upon the abundant mercies of Jesus for our life and the lives of those in need. Grant that we may choose to drench ourselves in the blood of the Lamb, acknowledging the price Your Son paid to cleanse us from all of our sins and to bring us to everlasting life. We ask You to share with us the mercy that awaits our contrite request, always trusting that it will be granted according to Your will.

Teach us, Lord, how to immerse ourselves in prayer and meditation. Help us to understand the suffering of Your people upon this Earth and how we can best support them. We ask that the Holy Spirit perfect our humble prayers, making them pleasing to You.

Also, gracious God, accept our suffering as well as our joy as an offering to You; trusting that our journeys be filled with both. Help us to embrace the cross You chose for us to carry and please remind us frequently that Your eyes behold a different kind of beauty. The wounds of Earth will heal but the scars are left because You cherish them.

Ignite in us a fire for the holy Sacraments and the teaching of the church You founded, that they might lead us closer to You.

In your precious Son's name we pray, Amen!

Seventh Prayer: The Piercing of Jesus' Side

The prayer of St. Bridget for the Piercing of Jesus' Side

Pray 1 Our Father, 1 Hail Mary, then:

Eternal Father, accept as worthy, for the needs of the Holy Church and as atonement for the sins of all Mankind, the Precious Blood and Water which poured forth from the Wound of Jesus' Divine Heart. Be gracious and merciful toward us. Blood of Christ, the last precious content of His Holy Heart, wash me of all my and others' guilt of sin! Water from the Side of Christ, wash me clean of all punishments for sin and extinguish the flames of Purgatory for me and for all the Poor Souls. Amen.

In conclusion

You are now invited to continue seeking meditative graces through the Lamb of God. Let not a day go by he does not hear from his one-of-kind and invaluable treasure. Open wide the conduit from Heaven to Earth by allowing Jesus' example to live on inside your heart, radiating warmth and compassion to those around you. Each and every person has the capability to make a difference, but it must be done while we still reside in this space called Earth.

It might be that the best shot a person has at glimpsing the love of Jesus is . . . by seeing or knowing you. God's "want ad" page is overflowing with job opportunities. You can easily pick up a part-time or full-time task. The benefits are truly divine and eternal. And guess what? You just happen to have the perfect set of qualifications needed for the job. God is counting on you and we all need you. Do us all a favor—answer your call! No one can do it like you can.

It's for you!

God bless,
Beth

Sources and References

The Circumcision, chapter 1

1-1. Dr. Alan Bercovitz is a board-certified medical doctor specializing in family practice. He is currently part of the St. Vincent Health Network in Indianapolis, Indiana. I was introduced to him through his lovely wife, Jeanine, whom I met during a Bible Study at St. Luke Parish, Indianapolis. My thanks go to both Alan and Jeanine for their help in understanding the ritual of Circumcision and its relevance to Christian baptism.

1-2. Website: http://www.behindthename.com was used in May of 2011 for the background and meaning of names and was included with permission from Mike Campbell.

The Suffering on the Mount of Olives (Agony in the Garden), chapter 2

2-1. Strobel, Lee. *The Case for Christ, A Journalist's Personal Investigation of the Evidence for Jesus.* Grand Rapids, Michigan: Zondervan, 1998. Print.

2-2. Wilson, Ian. *Murder at Golgotha, Revisiting the Most Famous Crime Scene in History.* New York, N.Y: St. Martin's Press, 2006. Print.

2-3. Strobel, Lee. *The Case for Christ, A Journalist's Personal Investigation of the Evidence for Jesus.* Grand Rapids, Michigan: Zondervan, 1998. Print.

The Flogging, chapter 3

3-1. For the scourging practices, Http://the-crucifixion.org/ On the physical Death of Jesus Christ, Scourging. March 1, 2010.

Also, Wilson, Ian. *Murder at Golgotha, Revisiting the Most Famous Crime Scene in History.* New York, N.Y: St. Martin's Press, 2006. Print.

Beth Leonard

The Crowning of Thorns, chapter 4

4-1. Henry, Matthew. *Matthew Henry's Commentary in one Volume.* Grand Rapids, Michigan: Zondervan, 1961. Print.

4-2. Mike Leonard, Feature Correspondent for NBC Today (NBC News) from 1980-2012 and is the Author of the New York Times Best Selling book *The Ride of Our Lives—Roadside Lessons of an American Family.* I met Mike at Immaculate Heart of Mary parish in Indianapolis, Indiana when he was promoting the book and video series *Catholicism.* I am grateful to Mike for his contribution to this chapter.

The Crucifixion, chapter 6

6-1. Chacon, Rev. Frank and Burnham, Jim. *Beginning Apologetics 1, How to Explain and Defend the Catholic Faith.* Farmington, New Mexico: San Juan Catholic Seminars, 1993-2004. Print.

6-2. United States Conference of Catholic Bishops web site, Article, Celebrating the Mass through the Ages by Norbertine Father Alfred McBride. As of February, 2014: http://www.usccb.org/beliefs-and-teachings/how-we-teach/catechesis/catechetical-sunday/eucharist/upload/catsun-2011-doc-mcbride-celebrating.pdf

6-3 Chacon, Rev. Frank and Burnham, Jim. *Beginning Apologetics 1, How to Explain and Defend the Catholic Faith.* Farmington, New Mexico: San Juan Catholic Seminars, 1993-2004. Print.

The Piercing of Jesus' Side, chapter 7

7-1. Website: http://www.catholic-forum.com was used for the information and story of St. Longinus, The Golden Legend, The Life of Saint Longinus. Information gathered September of 2013.

7-2. Website: http://www.catholic.org for information on St. Longinus, 1st Century Martyr, St. Longinus. Information gathered September of 2013.

7-3. Website: http://www.newadvent.org for information and history of Holy Water.

7-4. Kowalska, Saint Maria Faustina. *Diary of Saint Maria Faustina Kowalska, Divine Mercy in My Soul.* Stockbridge, MA: Marian Press, 2004. Print.

7-5. Specifically for the quoted prayer, refer to entry #186-187 found in Notebook 1 of: Kowalska, Saint Maria Faustina. *Diary of Saint Maria Faustina Kowalska, Divine Mercy in My Soul.* Stockbridge, MA: Marian Press, 2004. Print.

CPSIA information can be obtained at www.ICGtesting.com
Printed in the USA
LVOW06s0018080414

380701LV00001B/2/P